Climbing Out

An Adventure in Rediscovering Life After Loss

Bonnie Thies
Robin L. Flanigan

Copyright © 2023 by Bonnie Thies and Robin L. Flanigan

All rights reserved. No part of this publication may be reproduced without prior permission of the copyright holders.

For privacy reasons, some names may have been changed.

Book design by Katy Kuczek.

Cover photograph by Patrick Flanigan.

First edition: December 2023

ISBN: 978-1-7334101-2-0

These mountains that you are carrying, you were only supposed to climb.

— Najwa Zebian

*To Michelle,
It was the gift of your love and strength that
carried me through the unimaginable.
I love you to the heavens and back.
Love, Mom*

---

*To everyone else,
We all go through tragedy in our own ways,
often with some version of "I cannot get through this."
For me, even after a good bit of time grieving, I felt as though my insides were
going to implode. Eventually, somehow, strength emerged from within. I've heard
similar experiences from others. We don't always know from where this strength
comes…or do we?
Faith, hope, and love do carry us through.
—Bonnie*

Prologue

> *This is the Hour of Lead.*
> —Emily Dickinson

March 2005

I shout for Bill.

He doesn't answer.

His truck is in the driveway, the garage door is open, and the chainsaw is missing. He's supposed to be at a meeting at the Bloomfield Public Library, not cutting firewood. Besides, it's dark already.

I call out again. Still nothing.

I trudge to the basement to slip on a pair of boots and grab a flashlight, then pace the length of the snowy driveway at the edge of the woods. A gust of wind and I shiver.

"Bill!"

No response.

Shining the light between a stand of beech trees, I scream for my husband until my throat feels julienned. There's a weight in my chest, the kind that comes with foreboding. Bill was predictable. When he said he was going to a meeting, he went to a meeting. If he'd forgotten to tell me, he would've left a note on the kitchen counter.

I return to the house and dial 911.

"I just came home," I tell the dispatcher. I don't recognize the pitch of my own voice. "I think my husband is in the woods."

That's all I know, but the dispatcher asks questions anyway. Her tone is calm and measured. My chest heaves under my coat. I tell her what I know. It's Bill's job to feed the wood stove, and he had gone into our 18-acre forest at noon. I'd last heard the chainsaw while on a mid-afternoon conference call for work. I hadn't seen him when I left for an appointment around sunset, which wasn't all that unusual—but standing up his colleagues at the library? As board president? Completely out of character.

When the dispatcher has enough of what she needs, she says someone will show up soon and we hang up. There is nothing to do but head outside again. I sit on a stack of rough landscaping stones by the back door and pull up the socks that always droop inside my boots. After that I pass the time tapping my index finger against the flashlight in my lap.

Headlights flicker through the branches and I don't know whether to feel relief or dread. I hear a car door open and shut and then footsteps.

"What's going on?" a police officer asks as he circles around to face me. The question is routine and sounds like it.

"I came home from church and my husband's supposed to be at a meeting." The words echo in my head. "He was cutting down firewood earlier, and when I came home everything was still the way it was when I left."

"Maybe he's out having a drink with a buddy," the officer says, offering a two-finger wave to another officer arriving in a second patrol car. "Or a neighbor."

The first officer looks bored. I clench my teeth so tight my jaw hurts. "My husband doesn't go to bars."

The second officer, once he greets me with a quick tilt of his head, throws out the same theory, using different words.

I've been married to Bill for 27 years. I know he isn't at a bar. Shooting to my feet, I say, "Something has happened and we have to find him."

The first officer nods. "We'll get our boots."

I wait in the middle of the driveway and cross my arms to keep warm. The men are in no hurry. When they come back the first officer hikes a thumb to the west. "We'll start over there."

"I'll go this way," I say, pointing north.

I start walking, trying not to think about what might lay ahead.

Deeper into the woods the trees thicken and look ominous, their boughs snaking together as if protecting secrets.

I call out again but hear only sticks breaking beneath my feet.

I'm wishing I had on different socks when the flashlight beam lands on Bill. He's on his belly, his bruised face to the side in the thawing mix of mud and snow, and I know. Blood has pooled in his ear and around his nose and mouth. His right eye is black and bulging. Nearby is the chainsaw and the trunk of a freshly cut beech tree.

I bend down, close his eyes, and rest on top of him, burying my nose in the rough nap of his thick coat. I touch his hair and stroke his cheek. He smells like earth.

Minutes later, when shafts of light glint in the distance, I clumsily move to my knees to yell for the two officers.

"Help me." My voice is a weak warble.

I shut my eyes so tight I see more stars than glimmer above the treetops.

"HELP ME!" This time my plea shreds the air, shreds my throat worse than earlier.

"Where are you?" one of them hollers.

I point my flashlight toward the sky as a beacon, then hear the men thrashing between the trees in my direction. They try to pull me away but I grab at the dirt.

"I'm not. Leaving. Here."

The first officer pulls out his phone and turns his back to make a call. The second officer stands watch, resting his hand tenderly on my shoulder for a couple seconds every now and then. I don't mind. After several minutes he says, "Let me know when you're ready."

How will I ever be ready?

But the ground is cold, I am covered in mud, and there is nothing I can do to bring Bill back.

A police investigator is in my kitchen. He towers over the counter, asking question after question.

What family do I have?

"My daughter's in North Carolina." Michelle lives three states away.

Is there anybody he can call for me?

"My niece lives near here."

I give him Annie's number, then try to tune him out. I hear only snippets of his end of the conversation. He says the word "accident" and the phrase "come right away." I smooth a hand over the Formica countertop. When he hangs up, he wants to know where I was before I came home.

"Church." I already told him that. It dawns on me that he has to rule me out as a suspect. I'm too numb to care. Someone could hammer my hand and I wouldn't feel it.

But the mention of church this time makes me think of something else.

"We have to call a priest."

"Okay," the investigator says. "Who's the priest? And how do I reach him?"

"I have no idea." I don't know why I just said that. I know Father Mull well, and under ordinary circumstances could drum up his number by memory.

I look out the window. The driveway is lit by the moon and lined with cars. Officers are milling around. One is a woman and I wonder if she would've assumed Bill was grabbing a beer with the guys.

An ambulance arrives.

I pull a church bulletin from a stack of papers on the dining room table and hand it to the investigator. "Call Sister Diane at Saint Bridget's. She'll know how to reach somebody."

There's nothing to do but stare at the driveway until Annie gets here. With only nine years between us, we have always been more like sisters. I try to ignore the bustle while I wait. When her car pulls up I go outside, the investigator tagging along like an unwanted shadow. As Annie and I walk toward each other, I blurt out what has happened in a wild howl.

Don't cause a scene, I scold myself.

Then I scold myself for scolding myself. This is the precise definition of a scene.

Annie throws open her arms. I feel her shaking when we clutch. "What can I do?" she asks.

I don't answer until we untangle—partly because I don't know how to answer, partly because there is no answer.

I look down at my pants, covered in mud. "Maybe I should get out of these clothes."

We move inside, the investigator still close behind. Too close.

I turn around. My eyes drill into his. "I'm going upstairs to change," I say, my tone clipped and rude. On a normal day I would immediately apologize, but I feel no remorse.

I walk gingerly, careful not to get clumps of mud on the carpet. In the bedroom I pull an empty hamper from the closet. The struggle to get each leg out of my grimy pants and into a clean pair is exhausting, even more so because I know that when I'm done I'll have to make the hardest phone call of my life. I've waited long enough, and now that Annie is here, it's time.

"I have to tell Michelle."

My daughter and I talk almost every day, so she won't suspect something's wrong when I call. I'm going to break her heart. She'll probably drive up with her partner, Beth, and their three-year-old daughter, Katie, as soon as she hears.

Annie gives me a hug and we walk back downstairs. Ignoring the investigator—who I'm sure is watching me—and the people who have gathered indoors in my absence, I slip into the room next to the kitchen for privacy. The room where Bill and I usually drink bourbon and talk. I dial Michelle's number, the lights from the officers' cars washing over the room.

Michelle sounds perky as usual when she answers.

"Dad was cutting down trees," I say, getting right to it, and soon she knows, and after that there isn't much else to say.

"We'll get our things packed and head up." I can tell from Michelle's voice that she feels numb too.

Not long after, Father Mull arrives. He offers a hug and his condolences. Taking off his coat, he says, "You have a beautiful home."

"Thanks. We enjoy it." I notice the present tense and take a loud, deep breath.

"Would you like to sit down?" I extend my hand toward a chair at the now-crowded dining room table. In addition to Annie, who has been serving cups of tea, several nuns from Saint Bridget's have come to show their support, including Sister Dorothy—a nun I've grown close with in recent years. They all nod greetings.

Prologue

I finally begin to weep.

Throwing my hands over my mouth, I sputter through spread fingers, "What do I do now?"

It's midnight by the time the stretcher carrying Bill's covered body is moved out of the woods and placed on a gurney on the snow-patched blacktop.

The commotion has escalated. Aside from Father Mull and the nuns, four Ontario County sheriffs, the ambulance driver, a coroner, and an assistant funeral director now mill around. It's all white noise as I stand, blank and unmoored, next to the stretcher. If it seemed like a scene before, this feels like a downright circus. I don't know how my feet are holding me up. No scale would be capable of measuring my weight right now.

A nun approaches. "Would you like the final prayer right here?"

I nod. "He loved these woods. This is where he belongs."

I stand near Bill's head. The crowd forms a wide circle around me. A man from the funeral home who had been standing near me steps back, separates his feet, and clasps his hands. A purposeful, respectful stance.

I place my hands on Bill's chest, strong and solid beneath the body bag.

"I know you're in a beautiful place." My voice is barely above a whisper. "A grand and glorious place. I'm just not ready for you to be there."

Father Mull begins. "Go forth, faithful Christian, into the arms of the God who created you."

I feel the wind pick up and hear it pass through the metal chimes on the side porch, the chimes with the dangling stained-glass cross.

"Go forth, faithful Christian, and be at peace with your God."

The first-quarter moon is bright overhead. I hear Annie weep.

"In the name of the Father," the priest continues, making the sign of the cross, "and of the Son, and of the Holy Spirit. Amen."

Feet shuffle as the circle unravels.

I am alone.

Chapter 1

March 2008

Kilimanjaro International Airport looks dirty and dated with its dim yellow lights and low-slung roof. The African air, hot and humid, smells like something is burning.

I step onto the tarmac, arching my back and relieved to be off the plane after 29 hours of travel. A mid-flight brandy can only counterbalance so many bouts of interrupted sleep.

"Feels good to stretch, doesn't it?" Jim says.

We walk toward the building with almost 40 other hikers. Most of us are from Upstate New York, each hoping to summit Mount Kilimanjaro in eight days. Following Rick, a friend and one of the guides for our climb, we pass through a double door monitored by security guards in wrinkled uniforms. Sweaty people are everywhere. We wait in line for our visas, a process that relies heavily on what appears to be a sustained effort to move around stacks of carbon paper. After nearly an hour, we exit the building through a murky sliding glass door. The air is on fire again.

"Yusuf!" Rick's voice booms. "Did you miss me?"

A short man with a denim jacket and wide grin makes his way toward us. In his early 30s maybe, he has faint dimples and a sprawling goatee. The men hug. Rick had talked a lot about Yusuf, a Kilimanjaro guide, before we left home. They'd met eight years ago on Rick's second trip up the mountain, back before he was 50 and bald, back when he had blond hair the Africans liked to pull for fun. Rick knows Yusuf hasn't had a chance to miss him—he was here three weeks ago with another group of climbers.

Yusuf walks with a slight swagger as he ushers us to a parking lot edged with manicured bushes. Lines of Land Cruisers wait to take tourists on safari. The majority of us will be going on a post-climb safari to the Ngorongoro Crater, an ancient volcano believed to have once been as high as Kilimanjaro. Though the tourist attraction is a draw for lions, antelopes, wildebeests, and other wildlife, I'm much more interested in the umbrella-shaped acacias, exotic and graceful and different from any tree I've ever seen.

Unlike the mint-condition Land Cruisers, the two white shuttle buses for our group have seen better days. They're old, banged-up, and rusted. A mess of backpacks and duffel bags line the ground beside them.

Rick tilts back his head and sniffs the air. "Smell that? People are burning trash and greenery to ward off poisonous snakes and other varmints. Now tell me how many bags you brought."

One by one we tell him. He tallies the total, then counts the bags on the ground. The numbers don't match. He tallies and counts again, never breaking a sweat even though the numbers are still off.

"Not to worry," Rick says. "This happens every trip."

My eyebrows peak. What else happens every trip? I thought I would be nervous on the mountain, not standing in the airport parking lot.

Jim finds his bag—delivered ripped, its strap barely hanging on. After rifling through it, he seems satisfied everything is where it should be. He's more detail-oriented than I am, one of the things I've found so attractive over the six months we've been dating, so I'm guessing there's no reason for him to continue being concerned. Even so, I can't help worrying that something is missing.

Rick excuses himself to file a report about the lost luggage while our porters, in matching bright yellow polo shirts, pile as much as they can on the roof of each bus. What doesn't fit gets thrown inside through the back windows.

"All aboard!" someone shouts.

Jim and I find seats toward the back of the second bus. The air is stuffy, so a few of us open some windows, only to be hit again with the acrid scent of torched garbage. Good thing Rick returns soon with a thumbs-up signal and the engine rumbles to life. I'm too wound up to sleep but don't feel like talking. Instead I listen to the overworked bus on the worn roadway as we make our way to Moshi, the capital of the Kilimanjaro region. Our hotel is there. I caress the medallion necklace a friend gave me for the trip and stare out the window, mostly at gangly trees in shadow and cement buildings in various stages of construction. Natives gather outdoors at plastic tables, beneath faint bulbs, to watch the traffic. Nothing resembles the Village of Bloomfield where I live, surrounded by woods, rolling hills, and stately farmhouses.

Almost an hour later we enter Moshi. The town, in the center of one of Tanzania's major coffee-growing regions, is architecturally dense and cosmopolitan by African standards but practically deserted this time of night. We pass only one hot spot— a throng of Muslims in a square, praying, led by a man with a tinny intercom. Yusuf stands up in the front of the bus to say that as far as he can tell, Africa's population is split pretty evenly between Muslims and Christians, both very respectful of the other's traditions. He celebrates Easter and Christmas with his Christian neighbors, and they celebrate Ramadan with his family.

When we get to the other edge of town, built on the lower

slopes of Kilimanjaro, the bus turns onto a dirt road glutted with potholes—a road that seems to have no end.

After a while Rick stands up. "We're not taking you out here to shoot you."

So we have that going for us.

I have known Rick for more than a decade. He co-owns an outdoor adventure company called Pack, Paddle, Ski with his twin brother, Randy. Bill and I took lots of trips with Rick. I trust him like family, though he can spin tantalizing tales of terror for days about his hapless adventures around the globe. Cape buffalo have stalked his tent. A polar bear once stood guard in front of the outhouse he was hoping to use. He has escaped from rattlesnakes and grizzly bears and spear-pointing warriors. He survived a plane crash. He has been mugged. He has lost maps, food, even people for up to 24 hours. The first time we went with him on a canoe trip in Alaska—we did that twice—a storm caused the sea plane that was supposed to pick us up to arrive three days late. While waiting we ate rice and oatmeal, the only food left, and listened to Rick's stories. He had been stranded several times before, once with his dad on northern Alaska's Killick River. Nearly out of food, they grabbed a calf from a herd of swimming caribou, sliced its throat, and roasted the meat for dinner.

The bus continues to bump along, almost violently. When we finally pull up to a black security gate, Maasai warriors in red plaid robes, grasping long sticks and spears, hustle forward to shepherd us into the spacious, well-appointed confines of the Springlands Hotel. The place could pass for a South Florida resort. Leafy trees, potted plants, and finial-topped lampposts line the tiled courtyard. The Maasai close the gates behind us, making it feel as if we're being protected from something. But from what? The real Africa? The Africa with scarred roads and tattered houses? I suddenly feel guilty for where I live and what I own.

Rick ducks into the office and returns with room keys attached to chunks of wood and strips of leather. He passes them out.

Chapter 1

"Come back here to grab something to eat after you drop off your bags."

I take note of the number on Jim's key. He's rooming with his friend Jack.

"See you soon," I say, then turn toward Sue, a short woman with close-cropped curly hair. "You ready?"

"After you," Sue says.

While training together over the past year, Sue and I agreed to share a hotel room and be tentmates on the mountain. We follow a stone path and flight of stairs to an end unit on the second floor. Inside the room, a green mosquito net hangs over a bed by the window—a bed that looks to be nothing more than a sheet of plywood with a thin foam mattress. More than 7,000 miles separate us from the comforts of home, and in this moment I feel the distance of every one.

I give Sue a sideways glance and snicker. "We're not in Bloomfield anymore."

At least our accommodations are spacious enough, with two mustard-yellow bedrooms and a bathroom.

"I'll take this one," I tell Sue, carrying my bag into the back bedroom.

"Sounds good," Sue says. Her bag lands on the mattress with a thud. "I'm going downstairs to eat."

Interesting. She's not going to unpack? Usually on trips I unpack right away. Maybe I should switch things up a bit and head downstairs too. I'm tired and hungry anyway.

"Sounds good," I say. "I want to check out Jim's place first, so see you there."

Along the way, I pass palm trees, more manicured bushes, a pool, white roses, and red flowers that look like misshapen pinecones.

I knock on Jim's door. He answers right away, eager to show off his room. It's on the small side but he doesn't seem to mind. I'm happy there's not much to see because I'm getting hungrier by the second.

I put my hand on my stomach. "Let's eat."

We head to the outdoor lounge area packed with tropical plants. The stars are thick and luminous. Most of the group is already here, drinking Kilimanjaro Premium Lager and dreaming aloud about reaching the top of the snow-capped mountain on the label. After all this time, I can't believe we will be on the trail the day after tomorrow.

Jim and I order beers and tear into a plate of grilled cheese and tomato sandwiches. The second my mouth touches the lightly toasted bread, I wonder if anything has ever tasted so good. We ate on the plane but that seems like too many hours ago to count. I rub Jim's back and look from one table to the next, taking in the size of our group and our varying ages. The youngest hikers are in their 20s, the oldest in their 70s. At 57 I'm unmistakably less spry than the young ones, but nimble enough. We have helped one another train on trails in the sun, mud, and snow—even after an ice storm on the side of a mountain, the ice-packed branches making us feel as if we'd been dropped into a fairy tale. We're all connected in some way by cancer. That connection is why we are climbing Kilimanjaro—as a fundraiser for cancer research. Some of us have been diagnosed and treated. Some, like myself, twice. Others have watched the disease ravage someone close to them. That's the case with Kim, a woman in her 30s who never goes anywhere—not even on a mountain-climbing trip—without large hoop earrings. She has brought the ashes of her father, who died of lung cancer, to release at the top of the mountain.

My Kilimanjaro Premium Lager arrives just as I'm finishing my sandwich. I ordered it because of the name, since I'd take a whiskey or brandy over a beer any day. The lager is decent but I'm more than ready for bed before I can finish the bottle, so while some order another round, I take one last sip and kiss Jim goodnight.

Chapter 1

"No one needs to be carrying me to my room," I tell the group. "I'm heading up. See you in the morning."

"I'll be up soon," Sue says.

I'm so tired it takes work to climb the stairs back to the room.

What does this say about my readiness for the gargantuan climb ahead?

I brush my teeth with bottled water supplied by the hotel since the tap water isn't safe for drinking. Once in pajamas, I slip under sheets cooled by an overhead fan, then tuck the edges of the mosquito net under the mattress and behind my pillow, making sure there are no gaps.

The net makes me feel like a caught cod.

Though grateful to have met Jim, I can't help thinking Bill would be here with me if things had been different.

Drifting off to the hum of the fan, the words I wrote to Bill on the airplane run like ticker tape behind my eyes: *I miss you and wish we could've made this trip together. But you've put me in such good hands. I know you're watching over me.*

Chapter 2

After everyone left the night of the accident, I fell onto the left side of the bed—my side of the bed—fully clothed. I stared out the window at the moonlit fir trees in the front yard. Bill's barrel-chested body usually blocked part of my view, but there was only a picture-perfect expanse before me. I smelled his pillow, flailed my arm across the mattress, and flopped from my stomach to my back, failing to find comfort in a familiar place that had turned brutally unfamiliar.

I fell asleep by 3 a.m. but awoke two hours later with a throbbing head, seized with a fear that friends and neighbors would hear about the accident on the news. Exhausted, I slithered out of bed. The bottoms of my feet, scuffing the floor, sounded like slippers as I dragged myself into the bathroom. I pulled out the top drawer of the vanity for my toothbrush.

It was next to Bill's toothbrush.

His things were going to be everywhere.

Trying to tamp down the panic, I turned brushing my teeth into a series of mechanical steps: Take toothbrush out of drawer. Squeeze toothpaste onto bristles. Put bristles in mouth. Brush. Rinse.

Chapter 2

Walking through the bedroom on my way downstairs, I noticed a pair of Bill's pants hanging on the back of a chair and his flashlight on the nightstand.

How was I supposed to reconcile this great loss while being surrounded by things that proved he was just there?

The flip of the light switch echoed in the kitchen, seemingly emptier than it had ever been. My swollen eyes fought to adjust. I grabbed a notebook and pen and sat at the counter, making a numbered list of people to call and noting those I needed to catch before they left for work. Done with the list before sunrise, I lapped the house aimlessly. I stopped to run my fingers against Bill's leather wallet on his desk, then picked up one of his favorite coffee mugs, the one with the mosaic Aztec sun god, next to the sink. I didn't want to put down the mug—my hands were touching where his hands had been less than 24 hours earlier—so I carried it around with me as I continued my laps. The suspense novel Bill had been reading lay on the dining room table, next to his *Field & Stream* and *Backpacker* magazines. In the piano room, the pillow on the rocking chair was still crumpled from his back.

When dawn finally arrived, it felt like an entire day had passed.

About an hour later I picked up the phone and called Joan, a neighbor across the street.

"You probably saw all the police cars here last night," I said.

"No, why?" Joan's voice was lively.

Oh Lord, I thought, I can't do this.

Fifteen minutes later she was on my doorstep with a plate of orange slices and chocolate chip cookies pulled from the freezer. I accepted the handout but not what had happened, losing my husband quick as a clap.

Michelle, Beth, and Katie arrived by early afternoon the next day. "Grampee's not here," Katie said in her toddler voice.

I rubbed her shoulder. "Grampee's in heaven."

Katie beamed. "He's drinking coffee with God."

I kissed the top of her head, sniveling quietly because Bill wouldn't see her grow up.

Katie slept in my bed that night. I stroked her hair even after she had fallen asleep, remembering the picture on my refrigerator taken when she was three months old and I'd just finished chemotherapy—our bald heads touching. When my hair first started falling out, Bill had wanted to be helpful. He'd read someplace that Duct tape could speed up the process. I was reluctant. A nurse had equated the soreness I was feeling already—the soreness that comes when hair follicles open enough for the strands to wiggle awhile before letting go—to a loose tooth. Duct tape seemed so savage. I gave him permission to try a small piece of masking tape instead. The rip was painless, even pleasurable. I approved moving to the stronger stuff and for a week that was our nightly ritual, pieces of me being torn away until there was nothing left on my head to take. Without Bill, I felt as if my heart had been torn away. A sideways sleeper, Katie nudged me into a corner and kicked much of the night, but I was glad to have someone to lay beside.

Days later I was on my own again.

I talked to Bill the moment I woke up. *Only six days ago you were here. Only seven days ago you were here.*

I gave myself instructions for the most minor of movements. Even the voice in my head was a drawl from the exhaustion.

Swing your legs off the bed, put your feet on the floor.

Comb your hair.

Eat something.

The house wasn't completely quiet because of our three cats,

Chapter 2

who got more of my attention than usual and gave me a reason to talk out loud. Sometimes I asked if they missed their dad. There hadn't been enough room in Bill's obituary—crowded with a nod to his service in the U.S. Air Force and other standard biographical information—to include how he'd lined the rotted dip of a fallen tree trunk with leaves so the cats could curl up there.

Every night I tried not to replay what I saw in those woods.

How could I not replay what I saw?

The idea of "losing" my husband didn't resonate. Losing something implied that it could be found, the way coins turned up between couch cushions or at the bottom of a purse. My life partner had been stolen from me. Forever. No amount of searching would change that.

As a girl, my second-floor bedroom overlooked a giant crabapple tree. Year after year, when the buds burst into five-petaled blooms that veiled the yard in pink clouds, I'd throw open my arms and recite, "I live in the best country in the world! I live in the best state in the world! I live in the best town in the world! I live in the best house and I have the best room in the world!"

I couldn't see the best in anything anymore.

I woke up alone. I sat alone. I drove alone. I read alone. I watched TV alone. I walked through the house alone. I cried alone. I went to bed alone. When I called a neighbor up the street to come over because I saw a mouse in the basement, I cried—upset for having to make the call, upset that I was breaking down, upset that I didn't know how to replace water filters or where Bill stored the extra cat food.

Morning prayers were rote. Saying the rosary brought some comfort, as did thumbing through memorial prayer cards tucked between the thin pages of Bill's rust-colored Bible. One of the prayer cards was for Pope John Paul II, who died 12 days after Bill's accident. The incessant news coverage was a welcome distraction. I spent the weekend staring at the television, absorbed in a universal mourning that took some of the edge off my personal grief. I wasn't the only one feeling gutted—a tiny consolation in that gauzy haze, toggling between the before and the after and feeling a constant need to recalibrate. That weekend I wrapped myself in one of Bill's fleece shirts and wrote him a note: *You already know that Pope John Paul II died. Maybe you needed to be there first to help prepare something for him. I'm sure whatever it was, you did it perfectly.*

I ate salads almost every day because they were easy. Open fridge, toss greens in bowl, top with leftovers. I ate and still felt hollow. On listless nights at the computer I'd pick up one of Bill's knives lining the edge of the keyboard. His knives were all around the house. I could still hear him say, "You never know when you might need one."

An orderly life became irrelevant. I no longer cared that the bills in my wallet were out of numerical order, or whether every shirt in my closet faced to the left. I ignored open newspapers on the floor, and left shoes where I kicked them off instead of tucking them away neatly in the closet. I lost 20 pounds in two weeks, my sunken cheeks making me look the way I did during chemotherapy.

I despised the way people saw me—as a widow. That sort of news doesn't stay secret for long in a small town. Even with people I didn't know, I could see in their eyes that they knew.

The idea of having to work right after the accident was barbaric so I took three weeks off, though even after that I wasn't ready to return. At least I never had to wonder what to wear on the job. All my suit jackets were the same, from Land's End, in different colors. Every day I paired one of them—each appearing to grow in size as I shrunk—with a turtleneck and matching pants.

In spite of the fact that I did the same thing every day as a technical sales engineer—demonstrating why companies like Xerox and Motorola needed highly complex engineering testing and measurement equipment—my job for the first time felt monotonous. I'd always liked thoroughly researching and documenting talking points well before each meeting, hoping to coax a client into a sale. I'd even rehearse one last time on my way to an appointment. Those first days back at work, however, there had been no research, no structured talking points. It had taken every ounce of effort just to glance at a few notes in the parking lot. Instead of admiring picturesque farmhouses and grazing cattle along the commute like usual, my attention veered to the subtle factory stench fringing my territory from Rochester to Buffalo. Every now and then I reached for the radio, my hand resting on the power button for a few seconds before returning to the steering wheel. Not enough time had passed for music.

I couldn't stop thinking about the retirement notice I had given two weeks before Bill died. Our new snowshoes in the basement didn't help. We'd ordered them two weeks before the accident, wanting to get into the sport more seriously. Every time I went into the basement to do laundry I was reminded that wasn't going to happen—and that retirement would have to wait. Long ago Bill and I had carefully strategized our early retirement together, but after working with the same company for more than 30 years, he was laid off. After his weekslong search for a new job bore no fruit, we needed a new plan. I lit homemade candles and told him how much I loved having him home. I pointed out that we'd been able to spend more evenings together and that it had been easier for me to unwind on the weekends. I'd gotten used to popping out of my home office on weekdays for dinner that he'd prepared, then returning to my desk to finish up the day's work while he cleaned up. I didn't bring up how his job had stressed him out, or how he'd had to go on medication to lower his blood pressure. I did emphasize that, as a senior salesperson, I made good money and we could afford to live on one income. "It's your decision," I told him, "but just think about retiring now." He already felt guilty about being laid off. His grandmother, a strong woman who grew up in Austria during World War II, had raised him with the philosophy that a man worked to take care of his family. But after many long conversations, he agreed to retire first. When I described our arrangement to colleagues—that aside from cooking, Bill had taken on all the shopping, cleaning, and laundry, and sent me off to work each morning with a homemade lunch—one of them said I was lucky to have a wife.

On those drives between appointments, furious at the factory reek, I thought about how I didn't have a wife or a husband anymore.

Thankfully my customers didn't seem to notice when I hesitated and second-guessed at meetings. They told me I was one of their favorite salespeople, while secretly I wished I'd get laid off. I was tired of sitting in conference rooms, listening to people's professional problems, and wanting to cut them off with a terse "So what do you need?"

Under my clothes I wore the Saint William medallion necklace a nun had given Bill when he converted to Catholicism. I liked feeling it cling to my collarbone.

At night I talked to Bill in my journal:

> *I miss you taking all the pictures.*
> *I miss watching you drink your coffee.*
> *I miss the way you folded my underwear.*

For weeks the house brimmed with food, foliage, and flowers. People sent Mass cards, brought boxes of donuts, and made donations in Bill's name to the church and library, some from co-workers I didn't know that well. I kept a list of everything everyone had done for me. It became overwhelming just to look at it.

There had been so much to do. Pick out a cemetery plot, order a tombstone, send out countless copies of Bill's death certificate to put bills and the truck in my name. I processed none of it, moving through the motions on autopilot. The funeral home sent a green folder packed with what it presumed would be helpful information. I leafed absentmindedly through brochures and passed entirely on a booklet titled "Guidelines for Life Beyond Loss." I didn't feel beyond anything, only confined by a grief that made me feel suspended and flattened all at once. Sympathy card after sympathy card poured in every day, as did thoughtfully handwritten and photocopied prayers—enough concern to make the wicker basket holding them so heavy that the handle broke.

Then one day the mailbox was empty. I tried to be rational, telling myself there had to come a point when I'd truly be on my own. But that didn't keep me from kneeling on the carpet next to Bill's hamper to smell every shirt, every pair of pants he once tossed in with his coarse hands—hands I could still feel against my skin if I concentrated hard enough. I kept his magazines on the dining room table and bought chicken parts when they were on sale, using coupons clipped from the newspaper because that's what he used to do.

I miss pretending to be you and you pretending to be me, I wrote in my journal.

"At least when someone dies of cancer, you have time to say goodbye, to make your peace," my oncologist said about a month after Bill died. I fussed with the strings on my medical gown and thought about my older brother, Jerry, whose kidney cancer had metastasized to his brain the week he turned 50. He was given three months to live but made it through two-and-a-half years with the aid of some hardcore clinical trials. I had time to say goodbye to him. Bill's accident was too harsh in its swiftness. That's why, for so long, I would have a decent morning only to find myself slumped on the floor by mid-afternoon.

I was never mad at God, though. People kept asking me how that was possible because they certainly were. I could tell by their reactions that my answer was too simple, but I honestly believed

Bill was in a better place. How could I be mad about that? Besides, deaths happened all the time. If I felt any real sense of unfairness, that would've meant I felt entitled and that someone else should've lost a husband instead.

On a night I couldn't sleep, I felt an abrupt urge to leave my bed and walk downstairs to my home office. As if directed, I reached my arm over the computer to a bookshelf and selected a book at random. My fingers flipped arbitrarily to page 40, to lyrics from a song by 19th-century composer George Linley:

> *Tho' lost to sight, to memory dear*
> *Thou ever wilt remain;*
> *One only hope my heart can cheer,–*
> *The hope to meet again.*

From that night on, whenever I needed a boost, I read Linley's words. They were sweet and fierce with hope.

I started giving myself permission to eat anything I wanted, which meant more milkshakes and sundaes than protein and fiber, and eventually gained back some weight. When a close friend, Marge, showed up at my door one afternoon with a rotisserie chicken and sweet potatoes, I watched her open one drawer after another in search of a knife. I could have told her where to find one but didn't. I liked watching someone work in the kitchen again.

I resumed piano lessons and tinkered with the dulcimer Bill made for me, even though I hadn't played it in years. I chose new photos of Bill to replace old ones on the dining room wall—one from a hike in North Carolina, his foot resting on a rock, another from the Adirondack Mountains in which he's consulting a map near an old railroad track. I gave a copy of the picture from North Carolina to Sister Diane for All Saints' Day, when framed images of deceased relatives encircled the congregation. She put it on the windowsill across from the pew I sat in every Sunday.

People gave me books but I read only those that did not advise how to move past my misery and start life anew. I began a novel about a woman who moves to an island after the sudden death of her husband—I could relate to that—but put it down when the woman wound up with another man. That was why it was fiction, of course. I couldn't imagine someone else in my life, in my house, in my bed.

Chapter 3

The African night gently breaks with the sustained intonations of Islam's call to prayer, the first of five daily calls from the minarets of the mosque a few streets behind the hotel.

I wake to the foreign sounds and hear voices outside the bathroom window. I hop out of bed to look. Chatty women wearing brightly patterned dresses and gracefully balancing baskets on their heads follow a path of power lines on the other side of a wall that surrounds the hotel. The wall seems more like a barricade than a decorative divider. I don't like the way it makes me feel, as if my privilege needs to be safeguarded.

Maybe the privilege itself is causing the discomfort. The women's feet are bare and dusty, while in my bedroom closet nearly a dozen shoes hang in an organizer or neatly spoon in their boxes. And it's almost time to go to a breakfast that has been made for me. I have a feeling that a lot of what I take for granted will be made conspicuous on this trip.

Not wanting to wake Sue with the scratchy slide of dresser drawers, I fight the urge to unpack and—careful not to disrupt the piles in my suitcase—pull out only what I need. After quietly brushing my teeth, I meet up with a few other early risers in a narrow, open-air pavilion—another resort-style setting with black-and-white checkered flooring, green-and-white checkered tablecloths, and walls freshly coated with bright yellow paint. The food is waiting. There are sausages shaped like miniature hot dogs, crepes, an assortment of fruit, and ginger chai tea. Bees swarm the orange juice machine and jars of honey and jam. I fix a plate and sit at an empty table across from a small painting of Kilimanjaro, its size making the mountain appear rather approachable. I'm guessing Jim, an earlier riser than most, has already come and gone.

"Are my bags here from the airport yet?" The question comes from a 30-something named Mark. All I know about him is that he sports a mohawk and lives in Pennsylvania.

"Mine, too?" echoes a young woman named Elizabeth. She looks to be in her early 20s. "All I have are two pairs of underwear in my backpack." I haven't had the chance to chat much with Elizabeth, but she seems sweet. She lives in New York City, and as a young teen informed her parents she was going to live and work in Africa someday. She has to be a good soul.

"Don't worry," Rick says. "Luggage that goes missing usually comes the next day."

I offer to lend Elizabeth some socks and someone does the same for Mark. By the time I'm finished with breakfast, the pavilion is packed and both of them have enough donations to last several days.

Just as I stand to take a walk around the property, a few hikers rush into the pavilion with a boisterous urgency. They're wide-eyed and talking over each other. Apparently, now that there's daylight, we can see Mount Kilimanjaro from the second floor of the hotel. I take one last quick sip of my tea and return my plate to the kitchen before speedwalking to the balcony. Phil and Sadie, a couple in their 20s, are already there, lounging in plastic chairs. Sadie had skin cancer four years ago, at 19. Her mother is a breast cancer survivor.

"Hi." I wave. "I heard…"

I feel a hand on my shoulder.

"Turn around." It's Jim's voice.

I twist at the waist and catch my breath. After 16 months of planning and a year of hard training, I get my first glimpse of Kilimanjaro. It's silhouetted against a hazy sky. Nicknamed the "Roof of Africa," the mountain is beautiful and not as intimidating as I expected—probably because we're too far away for any rational perspective. The haze makes the view look like a vintage photograph.

"This is why I love nature," I whisper to Jim. "There's so much of God's beauty to see."

It's hard to believe we will be standing on that fabled mountain tomorrow.

From our second-floor vantage point, we can scope out more scenery on the other side of the gate. There's a cemetery across the road, its handmade crosses lined in lumpy rows of rocky soil. Rice fields sprawl from there. On a dirt strip paralleling grassy railroad tracks, men and women, everyone barefoot, carry plastic gas cans, clay pots, and metal buckets on their way to collect water. Barebones bikes zoom past, some laden with yellow buckets carrying grass to sell to town residents with animals to feed. One rider, in khakis and a loose shirt open to his navel, transports a tall pile of gnarled firewood tied to a small platform behind his seat. There is so much visible effort here both in the landscape and in the tasks being carried out.

We spend the next hour on the balcony until Rick calls from the courtyard, "Hey, everyone! Come down here for a few minutes. I want to introduce you to your guides."

I'm not ready for the interruption but dutifully make my way downstairs and take a seat in a semi-circle of plastic chairs.

Rick holds an open palm toward three men. "You know Yusuf," he says. "And this is Saidi and Tom."

The men smile and wave. Each has been assigned to one of three routes we're taking up the mountain.

I'm on the eight-day Lemosho Glades route that approaches the Kibo summit from the west. Six days up, one-and-a-half days down. Kibo is the highest of Kilimanjaro's three volcanic cones. Unlike the other two, Shira and Mawenzi, both extinct, Kibo is dormant and could possibly erupt again. I'm not nervous about that, though. If it hasn't blown in hundreds of thousands of years, my chances are better than good I'll make it through the next eight days.

The Lemosho route is considered the most beautiful, with panoramic views from various sides of Kilimanjaro. That's a nice perk, but I like the route even more because it's the longest, making it one of the best for acclimatization. More important, it's the route both Rick and Yusuf will be on. The rapport they share and the allegiance they have for each other can only play in our favor in case anything goes wrong on the mountain. Yusuf was a young and inexperienced guide when he met Rick, but he had been fair to the porters, clear in his expectations, and able to handle more complicated situations than most of the other guides Rick had worked with. They've been a team ever since. I'm not sure what kind of complicated situations we'll come up against, but I read that acute altitude sickness affects more than three-quarters of the people who climb Kilimanjaro. In its mildest form it can feel like a hangover with headaches, loss of appetite, nausea, and other annoyances I'd rather avoid. More severe forms I hope to learn nothing more about include fluid in the lungs or fluid in the brain—both potentially life-threatening. We'll be escorted down the mountain at the first sign of danger, so I'm not worried. But I need to remember to take my first dose of Diamox right after this meeting. The drug prevents and reduces symptoms of altitude sickness by blocking an enzyme in the kidneys, making the blood more acidic. The brain interprets the blockage as a signal to breathe more often and more deeply.

A fair number of the more advanced hikers, including Jim, are taking the Machame route, which is similarly good for acclimatization but more physically demanding. All things being equal, I would've preferred the same route as Jim, but as a longtime serious hiker he needs more of a challenge than I can handle. We will see each other on the mountain anyway, when our trails overlap on the fourth day. Only a few are traveling the less scenic Rongai route. With its northern approach there's less time for acclimatization, but it's an easier path up because of its gradual slope.

Regardless of the route, we all hope to summit at the highest spot on Kibo at a place called Uhuru Peak—Swahili for "Freedom Peak."

Though none of the routes are technical climbs requiring helmets and harnesses, getting to the peak will be an extraordinary challenge. There's no way to know how the changing altitude, weather, and temperatures will affect our bodies.

"We will climb to a higher altitude than our campsite each night, then dip down to a lower altitude to sleep," Yusuf says. He explains that the zigzagging helps our bodies adjust to the low oxygen pressure and increases our chances of making it to the top.

Every route moves through five distinct climate zones—lush rainforest, sparse heath, dry moorland, cold alpine desert, and frozen arctic.

"It will be like traveling from the equator to the North Pole," Yusuf says.

This is what makes Kilimanjaro an ecotourism hotspot. Speaking of hot, it's February, which means we're right in the middle of a Tanzanian summer. We'll have warmer temperatures at higher altitudes and less snow to battle than at other times of the year. Once March hits, so does the rainy season when the southeast trade winds carry loads of moisture over the Indian Ocean and turn the trails into mud.

Tom, the guide for the Machame group, tells us he is a former schoolteacher. He has reached Uhuru Peak some 150 times and was the first African guide Rick went with to the top of Kilimanjaro. Saidi, a rail of a man and a guide for eight years, came up through the ranks as a porter, then assistant guide, then cook. Some guides like Yusuf have completed a national certification process through Kilimanjaro National Park. Yusuf began his work on the mountain as a porter and assistant guide for Tom. A lot of guides start out as porters, learning early on whether their bodies can handle the altitude before going through extensive and expensive guide training off the mountain. It would be difficult, if not impossible, to move up the ranks if afflicted by altitude sickness.

"Be careful about having a strong mind," Yusuf cautions. "Listen to your body."

"Talk to your guides," Rick says. "Learn about them and listen to them. If they say go down, go down."

I cringe at the thought of being told to go down.

Rick reiterates a concept he has been stressing for months. "Never pass the lead guide and remember, try not to predetermine your experience."

No one has to worry about me hiking fast enough to get close to the lead guide, let alone pass him.

"Now for today's excursion into Moshi," Rick continues. "I know it's warm, but no skirts for the ladies and no shorts for anyone. Only kids wear shorts here. Make sure your skin is covered as much as possible. And buy only from established shops."

Rick teaches us a few Swahili phrases in case we need them when dealing with persistent store owners. *Hapana* means "No." *Sitaki* means "I don't want it." *Baadae* means "Later."

"And know you'd be hard-pressed to find typical African souvenirs in an African's home," Rick says. "They don't have the money to buy that stuff."

Yusuf pipes up. "We think about food, shelter, cloth."

There's a heavy moment of silence after those words—the

pause drawing attention to just how warm it has become, to the beautiful butterflies feasting on pretty pink flowers, to the hotel workers' body odor wafting on a slight breeze.

"The people here hike for survival, not fun," Rick says. "They usually walk five kilometers to find water, five kilometers to collect firewood, five to 10 kilometers to and from school. A weekly salary wouldn't cover the cost of dinner at a nice restaurant back home."

Rick dismisses us with instructions to head to our rooms. He wants us to confirm we are taking on the trail only what we need and nothing more. That's easy enough for me. The packing list said to bring one coat so I brought one coat. Sue brought two coats and a medley of clothes and outerwear that, on inspection from yet another guide a half hour later, has to be seriously culled before the day's foray into Moshi.

I found out months ago how differently Sue and I approach a situation. She'd invited me, Jim, and a few other Kilimanjaro hikers over to celebrate Hanukkah. When I walked into the kitchen, some of the other guests were putting trays of latkes into the oven and unboxing menorah candles. While Sue ran around taking care of last-minute details, declining my offer to help, I hung back and reminded myself that not everyone has the kitchen cleaned up and appetizers ready for serving by the time guests arrive. I wasn't being judgmental. In fact, I wished I had a job to do so that I could feel useful. I didn't realize until later what a gift that invitation had been. It was a warning of the gentlest kind. On the mountain I wouldn't have the familiarity of Bill. I wouldn't have reassurance from Jim. I'd be paired with Sue, who I saw only on hikes and with whom I was growing closer, but whose practical proclivities I knew nothing about. And we would be sharing a small tent together. I'd have to be careful not to have rigid expectations.

Chapter 3

In another hour we're on a bus headed to the center of town. Wanting to be respectful and comfortable, I'm wearing a wide-brimmed hat with neck flap, lightweight hiking pants, and a forgiving polo shirt. As we head down the rough road, ricocheting against each other's shoulders, I stare at what had been cloaked in shadow the night before. Humble huts made of sticks stand about 6 feet tall, pounded into the ground at three-foot intervals. Thatched roofs are covered with thick layers of dried mud and straw. Children huddle outside in small groups and wave cheerfully as the bus lumbers past. The sweltering air holds a mixture of dust and peculiar scents—burning rice stalks, diesel, charcoal.

With so much to take in, it feels like we get to Moshi in no time. The town has a reputation for being the cleanest in East Africa, yet the dirt walkways between buildings are littered with plastic hangers, chunks of red brick, exposed wires, and trash being mauled by stray dogs.

I have been in seven countries, but never one like this. In Bloomfield, you can drive for miles and miles and see only open fields and tired barns, but there's so much going on here. The man at a general store mops a roof made of reeds and corrugated metal. Women swaddle small children to their backs. The message on a concrete wall surrounding an imposing church with turrets proclaims, "None to be worshipped but Allah: Muhammad is his prophet."

The bus pulls over at the edge of a bustling open-air marketplace. Potatoes overflow old paint buckets. Fruits and vegetables crowd squares of fabric on the ground. Not one person wears the same color combination.

Rick stands up. "Don't be rude. If people aren't wearing their best clothes, they don't want their picture taken. But you can take a picture when you make a transaction with someone."

We split into three groups. Jim and I, with about a dozen others, follow Rick and Saidi through a tangle of nondescript cinderblock buildings. When we stop at an oversized door, I wipe sweat from my forehead. Saidi takes us inside. The place is stuffy and reminds me of an abandoned school. Long hallways, cement walls, door after door. No signs instruct us where to go—even if we could read Swahili. We walk down one hallway, up three flights of echoing stairs, and down two more hallways before stopping at a metal door. Six combination locks have been opened for our arrival, some of which look as if they wouldn't prevent an African goat from breaking in. Saidi swings open the door to a dusty shop. We are welcomed by a bald man with a cane. His shirt is unbuttoned, his chest hairless.

Inside, we walk past gem charts stuck to stained walls with wide strips of brown packing tape. The man transfers cloth bags from a shabby briefcase to a high table in the center of the room, spilling the contents for us to admire. Blue and purple stones, dark and vivid.

"Tanzanite is a rare gemstone," the man says in unhurried English. He waves his hand over the samples like a *Price is Right* model. "Found only here in the foothills of Kilimanjaro."

"He has good prices," Rick says.

Prices are in shillings. Jim, a devout list maker, reaches for his wallet to consult the currency cheat sheet he made back home. A retired analytical chemist, he has always given me a run for my money in the details department. Even though Rick had sent out a lengthy recommended packing list for the trip, Jim had decided to make one of his own, broken into five categories, each with its own symbol. An oval represents what goes into his daypack. A star inside a circle signifies what gets packed inside the duffle bag the porters will carry. He also plotted the trip on a chart with daily elevation gains and losses. His methods may sound pedantic to some, but I find them insanely attractive. I'm a sucker for order and achieving maximum productivity with minimum effort. The first time I was diagnosed with cancer, my initial thought when I walked out of the clinic: They're so efficient here.

I have no need for loose stones, so I goad Jim's roommate, Jack, for fun. "Are you going to bring anything home to your wife?"

Jack's smile is sheepish, his voice soft. "Too expensive."

I persist. "You're taking this whole trip for yourself, and I'm guessing you picked up quite a few things that cost a pretty penny to get here. Am I right?"

Jack curls his mouth in sportive protest and agrees to look at a sample. The salesman hands him a pair of tweezers to study a pea-sized gem, then helps a hiker named Carroll select two oval stones he plans to have made into earrings for his girlfriend's sixtieth birthday. I know a little about Carroll, that he's a technical rock and ice climber who has scaled mountains all over the United States and Costa Rica. Someone told me his girlfriend has had stomach and breast cancer. He's here with her son, a Boston marathoner.

Jack turns his wrist for a better view of the tiny chunk of tanzanite, and the gem flies out of the tweezer's vice.

"Oh no!" he cries, then looks at me stone-faced. "Maybe I will be buying something here. I just won't be taking it home."

Jack drops to his hands and knees to scour the floor and ultimately finds the renegade sample, which he quickly returns to the bare-chested man.

Most of us leave the shop empty-handed, myself included.

Once back on the streets of Moshi, we're immediately surrounded by street vendors hawking necklaces, hats, and an assortment of wood carvings.

"Jambo!" the vendors shout, presenting their wares with outstretched arms. The greeting is similar to the English word for "Hello!" and is used only with tourists, not other Tanzanians. It was the first Swahili expression I'd learned from a friend who climbed Kilimanjaro years ago.

"Jambo!" we respond in unison.

Rick reminds us to deal only with established businesses, but Jim can't refuse a vendor who badgers him for several blocks. After slashing the price of a small animal statue every few steps—what kind of animal we can't be sure—Jim hands over his money and tucks the statue in his pants pocket.

The marketplace, where the bus dropped us off, has gotten more crowded. A man sitting on a box sells a variety of thick sticks advertised as toothbrushes. Another sells brightly colored powders he says will cure colds and make men "more potent." Some in our group want to know more about that but I'm not interested, so while they ask questions I snap pictures of pushcarts packed with sugar cane.

Not long after we continue our stroll, Saidi darts into a narrow alleyway to vomit.

"That's the second time," Rick says softly, leading us past a store window filled with dangling chicken carcasses. "Hope it's not malaria."

Tourists like us typically take medication to prevent malaria. I'd started mine two weeks ago. Because the mosquito-borne disease is common here—and the leading cause of death in Tanzania—chances are Saidi has had it before. I'm worried about him.

We follow Rick into a restaurant. Suddenly tired, I plop down at a table beside Jim. The ripped tablecloth advertises Kilimanjaro Premium Lager: "It's Kili time! Make the most of it."

The advertisement works. We each order a bottle and watch soccer on a grainy television secured inside a cage hanging from the ceiling. When the beer comes we order fish, sweet potatoes, spinach, a root vegetable called cassava, and ugali, an East African porridge made from cornmeal and water. Rick says ugali is like mashed potatoes but thicker.

I'm not uncomfortable here but don't feel in my element either. I reach for my medallion necklace, smoothing fingers over the tribal face scrimshawed on an oval piece of bone. I keep picturing the dangling chicken carcasses. Bill and I used to drive past a restaurant with a similar window scene on our way to the theater in Rochester. He would've wanted to sample one here in Africa. He never missed an opportunity to judge local cuisine. Once, as we meandered along England's South Coast shoreline, he lit up as we walked by a row of vendors peddling raw fish that looked to me more suspicious than appetizing. I can still smell the water.

I sip my beer. The calls to prayer resume in the distance.

Chapter 4

I met Bill when I was 25. We both worked at a large company that manufactured testing and measurement equipment for engineers. Bill repaired high-end computer printers, and I was in customer service long before I became a technical sales engineer. We started flirting at a summer picnic at a colleague's home on Lake Ontario. Michelle was five. Watching the way Bill played with her, I could see a future with him.

After that day, back at the office, I began making unnecessary trips to stack papers in a mail bin near Bill's desk and within weeks worked up the courage to invite him to dinner. He brought steaks. Michelle received the bulk of his attention, which was fine by me. Our courtship was low-key. We shared homemade meals and wended our way through overgrown fields and conifer plantations on lengthy rambles. In a nearby wildlife conservation area, we would spot white-tailed deer, cottontail rabbits, and, if we were lucky, wild turkeys. Simple pleasures—the satisfying crunch of a potato chip, the sound of a popping ember—made us happy.

Bill moved in a year later and proposed in bed on New Year's Eve.

We got married on April 15, 1978.

Chapter 4

"I do promise to be devoted in sickness as well as in health," we vowed to one another, "to be as close in sorrow as in joy...and will only be separated by death outwardly but never in our hearts."

All couples say that sort of thing when they wed, but none of it means what it winds up meaning when the sickness arrives, when death disconnects. When cancer comes and then it comes again. When a husband is there one afternoon but not that night.

Like with everything in our lives back then, we kept the ceremony modest. Invitations were typed on an IBM Selectric. Michelle and I wore matching skirts and blouses sewn by one of Bill's aunts. At our reception we ate cold-cut sandwiches and scalloped potatoes, baked beans, and whipped cream-topped fruit salad before cutting a three-tiered cake baked by one of my sisters. We spent our weeklong honeymoon going out for fancy dinners at different restaurants around town while Michelle stayed with my parents.

Two days after the wedding, we met with a lawyer so that Bill could adopt Michelle, who was seven by then. He wanted to be her father, even though he wasn't always comfortable as a father figure. Raised mostly by his grandmother, Bill had no relationship with his own father. The only constant men in his life were two bachelor uncles with a low tolerance for kids. Playing with a little girl was one thing, parenting her was another. But he got the hang of it and within a month of us living together as a family, Michelle referred to him as her dad.

Money that could have bought an engagement ring went toward a down payment on a two-bedroom ranch house in Honeoye, a hamlet at the north end of Honeoye Lake. According to Native American legend, the lake, shaped like a gnawed pencil, is part of a group of long lakes that make up an imprint of the Great Spirit's hand. That imprint is known as the touristy Finger Lakes region. We lived on the western side of the region, on the slope of a hill surrounded by 14 wooded acres. Almost every weekend in the fall, I packed lunches and snacks and the three of us headed outdoors for the afternoon. Bill would cut down trees on our property for firewood while Michelle and I gathered kindling and stacked logs in a wheelbarrow. We ate lunch in an overgrown apple orchard at the top of the hill.

We hiked as often as we could in the relaxing—and affordable—outdoors. More often than not, Bill and I would get lost on the trails and Michelle would wind up on Bill's shoulders, sleepy and ready for mint tea. In the summers we'd meet up with relatives at primitive camping sites around Western New York, dining on Dinty Moore stew and sleeping in our station wagon. Sometimes we shared an archaic, oversized tent that none of us were all that skilled at setting up, a chore often finished in the dark after work and a long drive. Once, we awoke to find we had inadvertently staked the tent in the middle of a dirt road, but that type of thing —the adventure of it all—was what I loved about camping. And the trees. When a log house in the woods came up for sale 16 years later in the bucolic village of Bloomfield, a short jaunt to the north, we snatched it up. Set down from a two-lane road, our new home had a gorgeous redwood stain and views of an 18-acre forest from every room in the house.

Though the early days were easy days for the most part, Bill and I each had come into the relationship with baggage and eventually needed couples counseling. Our therapist had us role play. First I said in a deep voice, "Oh, it's raining out there. Maybe we shouldn't go hiking today. It'll be dark and wet and slippery." He followed in an exaggerated high-pitched voice, "It's always a beautiful day. Just look inside me—all that sunshine in there will light up the woods for us even at midnight!"

With a bit of work, we moved past the tricky stuff.

Chapter 5

I sleep so well that I miss the first public call to prayer. This pre-dawn version has an important distinction from the day's other four calls. "Allah is most great" is how the Arabic chants always begin, but there's an extra line tacked on in the wee hours of the morning—"Prayer is better than sleep."

When I do wake up, an electrifying current runs through me.

Today I will step foot on Kilimanjaro.

Sue is still in bed so I get first dibs on the shower. The water pressure is dismal but I don't care. I'm grateful to have any amount of water without having to carry it for miles on my head. Once dressed I walk to the spot where, yesterday, I first saw Kilimanjaro. With no one around, the balcony feels like a private observatory. The mountain plays hide-and-seek with the roaming clouds. As someone back home once explained about the mountain, "When it's not visible, the space where it should be is somehow different than the rest of the cloud-covered horizon. It's like being in a pitch-black room with other people. You can't see them, but something about the blackness where they're standing is different from the blackness where they aren't."

Down below, hikers begin to filter into the pavilion for

breakfast. I'm surprisingly hungry despite last night's buffet. We'd been treated to what we were told was a traditional African meal of white sweet potatoes, rice, beef stew, fish, and ugali, and plum pudding for dessert. After what Yusuf told us earlier about how most people here have to think about getting their basic needs met, I couldn't help wondering whether we were noshing like nobility and may have been overly exuberant in expressing my gratitude to our servers. A few hikers had bounced from table to table with their cameras, showing off images and trading stories about their Moshi escapades. I'd watched and listened with heavy eyes, resting against the shoulder of Linda Number One. Our group gave her that name because there are two Lindas on the trip and she's the oldest. "It's like I'm two people," I'd told her. "I'm so fortunate to be here, and to be here with Jim. It's just that I can't help but think of Bill."

My stomach gurgles. I should get something to eat.

"See you soon," I say to the mountain.

In the pavilion I wave to Jim and load a plate with porridge, toast, and fresh fruit, and pour a glass of mango juice. I decide against ordering eggs. No doubt the manager again will present them personally on a plate covered with a domed cover, the service matching that of a five-star restaurant. But whether that's five or 30 minutes from now—the various wait times for our group yesterday—is anyone's guess.

"Saidi has malaria after all," Jim says when I sit down. "He went to the hospital last night."

I don't know what kind of hospital he's in, but I've read about the lack of training for triage and critical care workers in low-income countries. I hope he gets what he needs to recover soon.

Rick calls for everyone's attention.

"So for the ground rules," he says, holding up three fingers. "Everyone should carry about three liters of water per day. You want your pee clear and copious. We don't want to start urine checks. Also remember that you're part of a group. It's okay to be

Chapter 5

weird, but don't be so weird that it affects everybody else. Try to get the names of some of your porters. Learn a little Swahili."

I know some words. Aside from *jambo*, I'd practiced some other commonly used phrases before leaving the United States—*asante sana* for "thank you very much" and *lala salama* for "sleep well."

"We're still collecting clothing donations for Mark and Elizabeth, and I know most of you brought stuff for the porters," Rick says, his tone taking a serious turn. "Thank you."

Before we got here, Rick had urged us to bring extra supplies to leave behind. I brought money and socks. Rick has gotten pretty close with some of the porters over the years and doesn't hide his disgust that most Tanzanian trekking companies pay them a lousy six dollars a day. Rick pays an extra seven dollars and expects each climber to pitch in another ten, our combined coffers to be split among the guides and porters based on hierarchy. The men use their wages to rent rooms without water or electricity. The younger ones pay school fees for books and uniforms. And it's not unusual for Pack, Paddle, Ski to do even more. The office occasionally closes for two weeks at a time to build homes and medical facilities in Tanzania. During these trips, the tour company's automated email response ends with this: "Sorry to inconvenience you. Thanks for understanding that often helping others causes disruption in our own lives."

"We're going to walk very slow," Rick continues. "It doesn't matter if we get to camp at two o'clock or four o'clock. If you get to camp at two o'clock, all you're going to do is sit around and be bored, or get cold depending on the altitude. Yusuf and these guys have been on the mountain hundreds of times and they know what they're doing, so rely on their guidance up there. You'll be amazed at how much support they offer. You're going to need to wear shorts and a T-shirt to start. In addition to your water, carry rain gear and an extra sweater or fleece. Any questions?"

"What's the weather going to be like?"

I don't recognize the voice behind me, but I know enough not to go anywhere near that question. I'd wondered the same thing once in Alaska. Rick's answer back then had been swift. "One thing I can tell you for sure," he'd said, "there will be weather."

He adds a little more detail this time. "If the sun is out, it'll be hot. Otherwise, if it's cloudy, maybe there will be a little rain and it might get a little cool."

Everyone laughs. Point taken.

We get our itinerary. The Lemosho group, with Yusuf at the helm, will be the first to depart for Kilimanjaro National Park. The Rongai group will be close behind with new guide Coleman, who is replacing Saidi. Jim and the rest of the Machame group, led by Tom, head out tomorrow.

Rick answers a couple other queries about gear and topography, and we start to disband.

"Remember," he says above the din of sliding chairs, "we're on a journey. We want to get to the top, but how we live the journey is the important thing. Now let's get going!"

We have about an hour to collect our things. I've been ready since my shower, so I wait in the courtyard in my lightest-weight hiking clothes and sunglasses. I make sure, for the third or fourth time, that everything in my new daypack is in its proper place—not only my water, sunscreen, and extra layers, but a prayer Sister Dorothy wrote for all of us and the banner I'm taking to the top of the mountain. All the climbers have a banner, each covered with the names of people we know who are fighting cancer, have died from cancer, or are waging on after losing loved ones to cancer.

"We will bring these to a higher place," Rick had said when he handed out the blank banners and told us what to do with them, "to bridge the gap between our physical world and somewhere else —wherever that is."

Attached to the outside of my pack is the pin one of the hikers, Tom, passed out at the group's last training hike, a comparatively gentle walk through Mendon Ponds Park. The pin has a picture of our group's logo—Kilimanjaro at sunrise—encircled by the slogan,

"IT'S NOT THE ALTITUDE. IT'S THE ATTITUDE." Tom signed up for the trip after hearing me talk at a Bloomfield Rotary Club breakfast. I spoke emotionally about my conviction to climb Kilimanjaro after battling cancer twice and while continuing to grieve over Bill's death. In his 50s, Tom had never hiked in his life but had recently lost his mother-in-law to cancer, and that had been enough. He signed up immediately. She must've been very special to him.

I slide my fingers over strings of letter beads clipped with a carabiner to the front of my pack. In lowercase letters, the beads spell "courage" and "inspire." Michelle, Beth, and Katie made them for me to carry up the mountain. Their laminated portraits hang beside the beads, next to a smaller carabiner decked with beads that spell B-I-L-L. Bill and I had always made a great team, even when he was supporting me from the sidelines. He took his job as my trainer seriously when, two months after ending chemotherapy treatments, I agreed to walk 39 miles over two days with Michelle for the Susan G. Komen Avon Walk for Breast Cancer. I wanted Bill to join Michelle and me on that walk, but after researching the event online he declined. "I think it's probably better if just you and Michelle go," he said. "There seems to be a lot of pink at these things." Yet for weeks, every Saturday morning, he trekked between 11 and 18 miles along country roads with me, sometimes walking an extra three miles into town for a treat at the village bakery. The Saturday before Bill died we each chose a bulging apple turnover doused in powdered sugar. "I just took them out of the oven, so don't eat them right away," the bakery owner had warned. We set the turnovers on thick piles of napkins before heading up the street. Half a block later we exchanged mischievous looks. Warnings were for kids. We bit into the pastries with abandon, then snapped open our pained mouths to let out the steam.

"Picture time! Group photo!"

The announcement makes me jump. I shake off the memory

and coach myself into rallying. I hadn't noticed everyone gathering again, or the arrival of the same beat-up buses that brought us here. How did I miss all the racket? Someone from the hotel tosses cameras into the air to a colleague, whose legs are pinned between green plastic sacks on the roof of one of the buses. The sacks are presumably stuffed with our gear. I position myself next to Sue for a parade of poses.

Then a wave of panic.

Is my raincoat in my daypack? It has to be. I'd better check one last time, just to be sure, especially since we're starting out in the rainforest. I move away from the group and unzip my pack. It's there, right next to the banner—the same place it has been every other time I've checked.

"Hey there." I feel Jim's hand on my back.

I give him a long hug. I'm happy our routes will collide on the mountain two days before we attempt to summit.

"Kilimanjaro's waiting!" someone calls out.

I pull back and smile at Jim. We kiss.

"See you on the mountain," I say, then board the bus.

Chapter 6

I wanted to know, without a doubt, where Bill had been standing when he died. I knew it was about 200 feet from the house, but I'd gone into the woods as many as six times without being certain of the precise spot.

It took weeks to muster the courage to call the investigator, who would be able to give me explicit details. I didn't ask for a police report. It had been enough to read in the *Daily Messenger* that Bill had been struck in the head by a limb about 12 feet in length and eight inches in diameter. The newspaper story included an interview with a neighbor I didn't know very well. The neighbor, who described Bill as an active man, said he'd driven past him walking home recently from the village's main street and offered a ride. Bill had politely declined. "That would've defeated the purpose, I guess," the neighbor was quoted as saying. I was glad to know that had happened. I hoped to hear more new stories about Bill.

On the day of our appointment, the investigator knocked on the basement door. I thought that was odd—odder still that I'd even heard him—until I remembered it was the door he used the last time he was at my house. He stood with another man whose name I didn't catch because I was too distracted by their matching trenchcoats, like something straight out of *Columbo*. A manilla folder hung from the investigator's fingers. I could only imagine what was in there.

I shook my head. "I don't want to see pictures."

"No, of course not." He hiked a thumb over his shoulder. "Let's walk out there."

I pulled the door closed and followed the men without a word through the woods, which mirrored all stages of life as winter turned to spring—decay and death, restoration and renewal.

Along the way I mouthed from memory something Sister Dorothy had written and given to me: "Finally God said, 'Bill, come with me and we'll have a long talk, and you will have all the mysteries solved and all your questions answered and you will have fulfilled the reason I created you. Come, my beloved son, and enter into the joy of your life.'"

The investigator stopped at the stump of a beech tree and referenced his folder. He looked at the ground, shuffled through the photos, looked at the ground again.

"Yes," he said. "Bill died when this tree fell. But it wasn't the trunk that hit him because he was on the other side of the stump. A branch snapped off at the exact moment the tree went down. That's what broke his neck."

So an even more freakish accident than we'd thought.

"He would've been right here, between us," the investigator said.

It took a minute for me to process the strange sequence of events. I nodded and cleared my throat. "Now it makes sense."

Except that it didn't.

Chapter 7

The drive to the base of Kilimanjaro, through villages and farmland and sometimes along rudimentary roads, is expected to last about two hours. From my second-row seat, I hold my camera at the ready. As we leave Moshi, a shopkeeper diligently sweeps dirt into a straw basket before the start of business. Click. Jacaranda and acacia trees dot the sprawling countryside, as do fields of cabbage and sunflowers. Click, click. We pass skinny cattle, children chewing on sugar cane, and a few tractors plowing fields before the upcoming rainy season. Click, click, click.

Numerous partially constructed houses pay homage to the area's "build-as-you-pay" system—another reminder of the country's economic hardships. As we pass a construction project much larger than the others, I push the shutter button repeatedly to capture Tanzania's version of scaffolding—a crude, five-story mass of sticks held together with twine. Are there building codes here? The structure looks like a sculpture, more artistic than utilitarian.

Yusuf, sitting across from me, is confused. "Why did you take a picture of that?"

Before I can explain, a truck overloaded with passengers in its cargo bed, too many people to count, pulls in front of our bus. I raise my camera and take another picture. One of the female passengers waves abruptly, signaling for me to stop. I drop the camera into my lap, feeling rude and regretful and recalling what Rick said yesterday about when and how to take pictures of people here. This group is definitely not in their Sunday best. Embarrassed, I avoid Yusuf's eyes and am glad he's not pushing for an answer to his question.

I fidget, my feet rolling the trekking poles under my seat, thinking of the two Somalian families Bill and I had helped back home. Each of the families had come from a culture like this one before being ushered to a refugee camp in Sudan and then brought to the United States through a Catholic charity organization. The first family, a woman with five children, moved into a rented four-bedroom house on Bloomfield's diminutive main drag. I taught them how to use utensils so the children didn't eat with their hands once they were enrolled in school, and explained to the boys that they wouldn't be able to have multiple wives, if that was their wish, when old enough to marry. Bill was retired by then and brought them lunch while I was working. "I'm teaching them the importance of pizza and chicken wings," he would report with pride. Some evenings we both helped with dinner, demonstrating how to use napkins, pass food around the table, and stack just-cleaned dishes in the cupboard. When the second family—a husband and wife with two children under three—needed someone to stay with them the first night in their apartment, I volunteered. After showing the parents how to flush a toilet, I walked to the bathroom sink for a lesson there but was cut off by the mother. She gestured wildly toward the sink and in broken English raved about how wonderful it was going to be to have a place to bathe her children. Realizing she had no idea there was such a thing as a bathtub, I pulled back the shower curtain and turned on the faucet. I'd never seen such a revelation. Late that night, I was almost asleep on the fold-out loveseat when the mother walked into the living room and lay beside me. I wondered why she wasn't in bed with her husband. Over and over she said her family usually slept on mud floors and gushed over how beautiful the apartment was for her kids. We communicated as best we could for an hour before I moved to the other couch, leaving the woman to spread out on the closest thing to a mattress she'd ever slept on.

I admonish myself. I shouldn't have taken that last photograph. I take too much for granted. I should have known better.

"There's Kilimanjaro," the driver says, pointing. "The south side."

Thankful for the distraction, I slowly scoot to the edge of my seat for a better view through the wide windshield. The mountain is still far away, but it looks much different than it did from the hotel.

"It's…big," I say aloud. The observation is at once obvious and startling.

The bus turns from pavement onto a dirt road marked by a corner soda shop in the shape of an oversized Coke bottle. The shop looks completely out of place, but Coca-Cola has a reputation around here. No one from our group is hiking the popular Marangu Route, also called the Coca-Cola route because tourists used to be able to buy Cokes on that trail. Local rangers would supplement their income selling the soda to thirsty travelers outside dormitory-style sleeping huts. Once Kilimanjaro became a national park, all glass and plastic water bottles were banned. I've heard that the huts are still in use, offering comfortable beds and solar lights. I'll try not to think about that when falling asleep on the ground or fumbling for something in the dark.

We drive by banana fields and coffee crops and try as best we can to ignore the dust the tires kick up through the windows. We have to leave the windows open because of the thickening heat. The shrill sounds of recess float in as we pass a school where students run around in the dirt—oblivious to the heat—or enjoy the shade of a rusted metal roof. When the relatively smooth dirt road becomes a very rough dirt road, we stop for a bathroom break. The women head one way, the men another. I walk down an embankment and inside an outhouse. There's a hole in the ground the size of a salad plate—my first pit toilet. I've never used one and don't know what to do. Face the door like in the portable restrooms at concerts? Or turn the other way, which would give me more room to bend my knees? Though I'll be cramped, I decide on my usual stance—facing the door. I pull some toilet paper from the baggie in my pocket and squat.

Londorosi Gate marks the entrance to Kilimanjaro National Park, at the western base of the mountain. The welcome sign hangs from a crossbar between two wooden poles, making the place look like a dude ranch. Porters hoping for work line a splintered fence.

While Rick picks up the permits required to enter the park, we sit in clumpy grass with boxed lunches—spindly chicken legs, boiled eggs, fruit, and juice boxes. I'm about halfway through the meal when a man approaches.

"Leave whatever you don't eat in your box for the porters," he says.

I look over at the men, some of whom have walked miles to get here. Rick has said there's a nonprofit organization based in Tanzania that tries to improve the working conditions of porters, but these men don't appear to be benefiting from any socially responsible tourism. They look nothing but exploited and desperate in their ragged clothes and malnourished bodies. I'm not hungry anymore. I wipe my hands on my napkin and donate the rest of my chicken.

Rick whistles. "Time to line up!"

We need to enter our names, occupations, and passport numbers into a logbook before starting our climb. While waiting my turn I notice a sign spelling out eight rules for the park. In carved, yellow-painted capital letters, they warn against things like attempting to climb the mountain without being physically fit, and mandate drinking between four and five liters of water or fruit juice each day. Rule number six: "DO NOT PUSH YOURSELF TO GO IF YOUR BODY IS EXHAUSTED OR IF YOU HAVE EXTREME." Extreme what, it doesn't say. I didn't know there would be park rules or security concerns. How can I follow instructions if they're not even finished? I look around for Rick. He's busy talking with Yusuf.

Another sign says "REFUSE AND EXPOSE CORRUPTIVE PRACTICES, ADVANCES AND OR GESTURES." Where are the signs of encouragement? A humongous "ENJOY YOUR CLIMB!" or "YOU CAN DO IT!" would be nice.

In Bloomfield, once a week or so a white clapboard church near my house rotates inspirational words of wisdom on a lawn sign:

> *God never shuts one door before opening another.*
> *You have to get out of the boat to walk on water.*
> *The greatest risk is often not taking one.*

After Bill's accident, the sentences gave me something to hold onto when grit—whatever level of fortitude I could marshal to get through the day—gave way to gloom. I'm a big believer in signs, whether overt or otherwise. Shortly after Bill died, two water streaks appeared one day on the mirror above my dresser. At first I thought the ceiling was leaking, but there was no evidence of water damage. The streaks were about two inches long, one a tad shorter than the other. I rubbed my finger slowly against the wet glass and a thought came so fast I didn't question it. These were Bill's tears. They were an affirmation he was watching over me and that he was sad about being so far away. I let the jagged trickles dry into smudges. They're still there.

It's my turn to fill out the logbook. I see that some of the hikers have taken liberties with their occupation titles. Seems I'll be climbing with an astronaut, a rodeo clown, and a porn star. I pick up the short pencil. Seems *they'll* be climbing with the Pope.

A truck pulls up loaded with more porters. The way Yusuf greets them, I know this is the team Rick told us about—a tight-knit crew of six. With a large group like ours, though, Yusuf needs another six from the queue along the fence. The chosen ones hop down and get right to work, weighing our luggage to make sure we're not bringing more weight than we should. According to official park rules, the maximum weight a porter can carry is 44 pounds. The newest guys sometimes ask to carry twice that amount so they can double their wages, but Yusuf doesn't allow that.

"Over here!" Rick calls from a row of muddy four-by-fours that Yusuf charmingly calls four-times-fours. The Jeeps are carrying our food and tents. We pack ourselves into them to endure what turns out to be a bumpy, seven-mile ride through a wet pine forest sprinkled with patches of corn, beans, and squash. Most of us cover our noses with handkerchiefs tied behind our heads, the doubled-over fabric acting as a shield from the exhaust and dirt. We look like terrorists. When we stop at the end of a sloshy strip, we think we've arrived at the start of the trail, but we've stopped only to switch to sturdier Jeeps with camouflage roofs.

"It gets more rough," the driver says.

My belly churns with nervous excitement.

There aren't as many of these vehicles, so some porters stand on the bumpers and cling to the rails, while others follow on foot, carrying bags on a narrow path alongside us. It's easy for the porters who are walking to keep up, since the Jeeps have to go so slow from all the jouncing. I'm in the back seat with Phil and Sadie —our shoulders smashing from giant potholes hidden in the soupy mud. I feel like my sports bra should have been put through this sort of test before going to market. I try to look out the side windows instead of through the windshield. I don't want to see what's ahead but catch sight of an impending deep rut anyway.

I grasp the edge of the seat with one hand, slap Phil's knee with the other, and screech, "I swear to God, that seems like half the size of our Jeep! We're not going through that!"

We've traveled thousands of miles to get here. Are we seriously going to get stuck and behind schedule on the way to the trailhead? Fortunately, we do make it through—white-knuckled—our bodies colliding furiously as the tires drop into the gaping hole.

"Watch out!" Phil yells. "Someone just got pregnant!"

The porters on the bumpers laugh as eucalyptus branches scrape their backs. These drivers could make loads of money as Hollywood stuntmen.

Ten minutes later, at an altitude of 6,800 feet, we reach the Lemosho Glades trailhead. I'm so happy to have survived the ride, I want to kiss the ground. What this means for my tolerance going forward, I have no idea.

"Asante sana," I say to the driver.

The trailhead, a simple clearing, is sprinkled with poop. Very large mounds of green poop.

"Elephant dung," Rick says.

I knew we'd be seeing elephants at the Ngorongoro Crater, but I wasn't expecting them to be on the mountain. I hope they keep to themselves.

Aside from the elephant dung, nothing about this trailhead looks much different than the Adirondacks where I hike often. I'll take that as a good sign and ignore the fact that there's really no sliver of a connection.

Some porters have been here a while divvying up potatoes, carrots, fruit, and eggs on a tarp as if it were market day. Bordering the tarp are empty five-gallon cooking oil containers the porters will use for collecting and treating stream water at each campsite.

Rick calls for one last pre-climb picture so there's proof we were clean and rested before spending eight days on the mountain. Two guides, both named Mohammed, frame the group for the photo. One Mohammed squats and smiles. The other stands stiff, arms crossed and legs spread, without expression.

Click.

As we form our first line, I look at the start of the path at the edge of the rainforest and give myself a pep talk. You don't have to choose the path. You only have to choose to follow it.

Before taking my first step, I close my eyes and pray.

God, keep us all safe.

Chapter 8

On a lazy afternoon by the coal stove in my living room, I flipped through the pages of a Pack, Paddle, Ski travel brochure. Maybe it was time to think about going somewhere with Rick. He'd called a few months after the accident to tell me a man who'd been on one of our Alaska trips had stopped into his office and told him what had happened to Bill. Then he started calling now and then to say he was thinking of me. "Whenever you're ready for a trip, let me know," he mentioned on more than one occasion. "We'll take good care of you."

I knew he would. I didn't know anyone like Rick. He was capable in any situation. As a kid, he slept in his back yard under a tent of blankets, later graduating to overnights in underground forts he dug in the vacant lot across the street. In winter he made the three-mile commute to high school on cross-country skis, returning home with his long hair frozen. He spent summers as a camp counselor in the Adirondacks and was promoted to waterfront director even though he had no idea how to teach kids about recovering from a capsized boat. The night of his promotion he got his hands on a how-to book, studied the illustrations, and went alone to the lake to practice in an old whitewater kayak. By morning he not only knew what to teach, he knew multiple paddling techniques and how to roll the sucker over too.

"Thanks so much for calling," I'd always reply. "I miss you."

The brochure was a tease and a torment. The Grand Canyon's layered bands of red rock, Romania's rural villages, the Arctic's hot springs—each description stirred up my globe-trotting instincts while inciting a new wave of mourning. Bill and I used to read these brochures together. We used to go on these trips. Aside from Alaska, we'd been to England, Ireland, and Greenland with Rick. We'd also gone on some of his unconventional local explorations. On a torchlight canoe paddle along Canadice Lake, not far from our house, we'd dined on baby spinach salad with chicken breast tenders, pistachios, grapes, and feta cheese. That beat typical trail food. I was even sentimental over our first canoe trip with Rick, although it had been far from relaxing. We were paddling the Nigu River, a tributary of the Etivluk River on the north slope of the Brooks Range mountains, in one of Alaska's most remote northern regions. I was accustomed to being the navigator with much less gear on the much calmer Finger Lakes, so when the gentle rapids abruptly turned into a full rush, I got scared. In charge of steering from the back of the canoe, I could see the 90-degree turn to the left coming up fast but had no experience with any course-correcting rudder stroke that would keep us from tipping. Rick shouted directions from his canoe behind us, but it was too late to avoid the branch of a willow bush extending over the water. The branch smacked Bill in the head, and we both flipped out of the canoe into the rushing current. I popped out of the water immediately. It took Bill a few seconds to resurface—enough time to make me think I may have lost him.

Week after week, I'd been picking up the brochure only to put it back down. Nothing on the adventurous side sounded appealing. Camping was out of the question, though it was in my blood. Growing up, family vacations had been spent at campgrounds paid for with coins collected in a dark brown gallon-sized jar kept on the floor of my parents' bedroom closet. We would camp anywhere as long as my mother had access to a Catholic church. But now I could easily picture myself melting down while trying to set up a tent on my own—a task I'd always left to Bill and to my mom and dad before him.

I closed my eyes.

Bill has been gone 18 months, I told myself. It's probably time I signed up for something.

Romania didn't sound half bad. While more than 4,000 miles away, it had comfortable hotels, nice restaurants, and easy hiking trails. According to the brochure, a native Romanian named Sergiu would be the guide leading walks through various cities, medieval churches, and markets, not to mention the hillsides that inspired Bram Stoker's *Dracula*. I decided to give the trip—and myself, I suppose—a shot.

When I closed the brochure, a letter on the back cover caught my attention. I don't know why I'd never noticed it before. The letter was from Rick describing a chance encounter with a former client, a cancer survivor, on a recent hike in the Grand Canyon. Their conversation about life and death had inspired him to lead a group of people touched by cancer up Mount Kilimanjaro. He wanted to use the trip to raise money for the American Cancer Society.

A jolt whooshed deep in my chest. It was the same sensation I got when opening Christmas presents on the floor with my granddaughter—the gut-level knowledge that I was, in that moment, doing exactly what I was supposed to be doing. It wasn't the first time I felt a lift in my spirit since Bill died, but I hadn't felt anything near that profound—even if the joy lasted only two seconds. Recalling how my dad used to tell me to trust my instincts, I picked up the phone.

"Hello?" Rick said.

My heart was thumping.

"Count me in."

Rick arranged for a meeting of prospective Kilimanjaro climbers at a popular Thai restaurant. I had agreed to go and, weeks later, was halfway surprised I showed up. More than a few times since my initial phone call about the trip I'd felt the urge to back out. I had also committed to going to Romania in the meantime. Wasn't that enough?

This was the first time since Bill died that I'd entered a restaurant without close friends or family waiting. I recoiled at the thought of standing alone at the door, darting my eyes from table to table, searching for a familiar face. I hadn't seen Rick in more than two years. What if I didn't recognize him right away?

Luckily only one large group was there. I recognized Rick from the back, even though he had much less hair than I remembered. He jumped up for a hug when I reached the table.

"So good to see you," he said.

"Same here. It's been too long."

I smiled at the others and took the last empty seat. There were eight of us altogether.

"Let's order while we get to know each other," Rick said, looking around the table and smiling. "Tell everyone what brought you here."

One of the men scarcely raised his hand in an offer to go first. "I'm Jim." His voice was soft. He talked about Kilimanjaro as a post-retirement adventure, which made me feel better about climbing such a legendary mountain at my age. Next to me was Jack. He said the trip would add to his mountain-climbing repertoire and, nodding toward Jim, would be a good way to fight against cancer. I wondered why Jim hadn't mentioned cancer, if he'd had it, given the purpose behind the trip—and whether Jack had just outed him. Across the table, a woman named Sue said she'd had cancer. One by one we talked about why we were there, and why we wanted to spend the next year of our lives training for what would be, for all of us, our greatest physical challenge to date. When it was my turn, I took a long drink of water before sharing that I was a two-time cancer survivor, that I used to hike with my husband, and that he'd died suddenly.

"He would've wanted me to do this," I said.

In my head there was one more thing. He would've come along with me.

The usual expressions of sympathy came my way and with all the talk about cancer, I was transported to the night Bill learned of my first diagnosis. My voice had been flat as I stared out the bedroom window and relayed that a routine mammogram had led to an ultrasound that had led to a biopsy and then a small conference room. There a doctor held out a large brown envelope. "These are your X-rays," she said. "You'll need them for the surgeon. We'll have the lab report tomorrow, but I feel confident about what I see." I supposed that meant I had breast cancer. Bill paced the bedroom. "Maybe they made a mistake." The possibility that I had cancer did sound preposterous. Just seven months earlier we'd spent 10 days backpacking through Greenland. We had maneuvered over rugged hills and permafrost heaves with 45-pound packs on our backs. It was absurd that rogue cells could be wreaking havoc in my body when I felt so strong. I looked at him and realized for the first time that what was happening to me wasn't just about me. "I don't think they made a mistake," I said. We held each other and wept, and I assured him I would be okay. On the day Katie was born, the lab report confirmed I had invasive ductal carcinoma, the most common type of breast cancer. The tumor measured almost two centimeters. I would need a lumpectomy, four chemotherapy treatments every three weeks, and six-and-a-half weeks of radiation. Less than two weeks after the surgery, I went in for my first round of chemotherapy—an aggressive form called "the red devil" because of its pigment and fierce side effects. On my way out I picked up a prescription for anti-nausea pills, though the nurse had said most people didn't need them. I threw up an hour after lunch, and every 10 minutes from then on over the next 30 hours, with one glorious 20-minute reprieve. Each time I ran to the toilet, Bill waited outside the bathroom door. When I was done, he handed me a warm washcloth and sat on the toilet lid while I rubbed my face clean.

A communal cheer snapped me out of the past. The table was filling up with spring rolls, noodles, and steamed rice. Had I missed someone else's introduction?

Rick lifted his fork. "Dig in, everyone, while I tell you why I want to do this thing."

Months earlier, secure in his sleeping bag at the bottom of the Grand Canyon, Rick was thinking about the numerous, awe-inspiring moments he has shared with clients around the world. Those moments often resulted in profound physical and emotional changes. While praying to the star-studded expanse above, he began asking the questions many ask in middle age. What do I want to do with the rest of my life? What direction should my work take? How can I reinforce what is good in this world? The next morning, halfway up the canyon where the junipers and pines clustered more closely, he stopped to rest. A group of hikers on their way down did the same. One of them wound up being a Norwegian scientist from Boston who'd hiked the Grand Canyon with Rick five years earlier. He'd recently finished treatment for prostate cancer. "Have you ever thought about doing a hike with folks who have cancer?" the scientist had asked Rick. Over the next couple days, still thinking about the Norwegian's question, Rick clarified his vision for the future. He would lead a trip to raise cancer awareness. The landscape would have to be dramatic and physically challenging enough to push people beyond what they perceived to be their limit. Those people would be mostly cancer survivors, and each would pledge to raise at least $2,500 for the American Cancer Society. Kilimanjaro would be perfect. He had been there three times and knew the mountain would have a powerful impact.

Chapter 8

Rick picked up his water glass. "Life is short," he said, looking around the table to make eye contact with each of us. "There's an unending explosion of beauty all over the world, and I get the chance to share that. Every time I go somewhere, a part of me gets reborn as I watch other people experience new things. It reminds me of what is at the innermost core of everything—something deeper than sadness and pain."

He took a drink. "Now I'll get back to the story."

The day after getting home from the Grand Canyon, Rick called his friend Matt, who had been recently hired as regional vice president of the American Cancer Society's Eastern Division. He was hoping Matt would help coordinate the trip and, better yet, come along.

Matt had been writing a list of key words and phrases he wanted associated with his new work when he picked up the phone. The list had to do with what he missed from his days as a summer camp director, and already on it were "Adventure" and "Get cancer survivors exercising."

"I'm in," Matt said quickly after the pitch.

"No offense, but this is kind of a big thing," Rick replied. "I'd like you to think about it."

Matt's response gushed urgency. "Rick, I'm in."

"So this whole thing was kind of accidental." Rick paused his story for effect before continuing. "Or maybe not so accidental."

By the end of dinner, we'd landed on a name for ourselves—Journeys of Inspiration.

"We have 17 months to raise money and get people trained for the mountain," Rick said. "Who's going to help me get this thing off the ground?"

After Bill died and I retired—finally—I typically found myself helping to get things off the ground. People seemed to think I didn't know what to do with myself. "I'm alone, not lonely," I routinely responded. "I simply miss my husband." But because I despise turning people down, when the secretary from church asked if I could assist with a garage sale and a new spiritual support group for women with cancer, I priced items and scheduled meetings. When Serenity House, a home for people near the end of a terminal illness, needed volunteers for its annual gala, I solicited corporate sponsors. When the Bloomfield Rotary Club needed help with its annual wine tasting and silent auction, I set up and tore down tables and chairs. So after Sue said that, as a doctor, she could easily provide information on what shots and medications everyone needed before traveling overseas, and after Jack and Jim offered to provide food at some of the longer training hikes, I agreed to design and regularly update a website for our nascent group. I had no experience with websites, but what experience did I have climbing mountains I knew nothing about?

I'd heard of Kilimanjaro, obviously, enough to understand that getting to the top would be no picnic. But I could only vaguely recollect a picture or two of the peak from the news and couldn't definitively point to it on a map.

I was only halfway confident the mountain was in Africa.

Chapter 9

The reddish-brown dirt trail is steep and narrow.

"*Pole, pole*"—pronounced pole-ay, pole-ay and translated as "slowly, slowly"—is the watchword on Kilimanjaro. Broad-shouldered lead guide Mohammed, the one who'd stood stiff for the trailhead photo, had said it again and again in a gentle, patient voice before we began our ascent. The slower we walk, the better our bodies will adjust to the altitude. I have no trouble with our unhurried pace. After cancer treatments, I'd wake up with a limited amount of energy and try to make it last all day. I could move quickly and use it up by noon or move slowly and stretch it out until dark. That knowledge hadn't come easy. At one point I got so sick rushing to get back into the regular swing of things, I thought I'd have to quit my job. It got to be too much juggling appointments from Buffalo to Syracuse, carting around more than 30 pounds of equipment and having to stand for long demonstrations in front of people who asked far too many questions. Eventually I learned to take steady, deliberate steps—the way we're walking now.

Rick calls our lead guide "the human metronome" because his stride is a measured rhythm keeping everyone in time. I'm toward the back of the pack near the other Mohammed. Gap-toothed and cheerful, he is the sweep, the term used for a designated last hiker who knows the trail well and is responsible for making sure no one gets left behind.

The lichen is luminescent. It hangs from trees and clings to rocks lining the trail. Nice scenery, but the air is so hot. At just 200 miles south of the equator, my sweat glands are in overdrive.

Sue and Linda Number One walk in front of me. The three of us have grown close over the last year in part because we have a seminal moment in common—a cancer diagnosis at age 50. I like that Linda Number One, a research technician, laughs easily and with her whole face. The first time I noticed, I was telling her about a vacation Bill and I had taken to Alaska. I had to go to the bathroom, but with no outdoor privacy I'd asked Bill to hold up my raincoat for cover. When a flock of ptarmigan passed by, Bill turned to watch them—inadvertently moving the raincoat and exposing me to the rest of the group. Linda tossed back her head, laughing, and said, "I'll be happy to hold your coat anytime you need me."

The three of us have logged a lot of miles together. Soon after signing up for the climb, I sketched out a six-mile walking route near my home. In the foothills of Bristol Mountain, the route was a challenging morning workout finished in time for a quick shower before my weekly piano lesson. Wanting company after a month of walking by myself, I emailed an invitation to the Journeys of Inspiration group to join me. By this time we called ourselves by our acronym—JOI. Both Sue and Linda Number One were there the next week. Each Friday morning, along with a handful of retirees and professionals with flexible work schedules, we turned out of my driveway, mostly in pairs, and headed up a small hill. My backpack was stuffed with a 10-pound bag of cat litter, the way Bill's had been while mowing the lawn in preparation for Greenland. By the time we reached the second hill, just under a mile, the hikers had already spread out some. Along the second mile we'd rest. At the three-mile mark, a metal gate flanked by old farm equipment and bushes was our turnaround spot and perfect for discreet bathroom breaks. We were usually quiet and contemplative by that point.

After a few weeks passed, on the way back to my house, I was watching the streams that had formed on the side of the road after a hard rain when Sue's voice broke the silence from behind.

"Do you want to be my tentmate?"

Sue sidled up after her question. She kept her eyes on the road and her hands around the straps of her backpack weighted with books.

I hadn't given any thought to sleeping arrangements on the mountain.

"Sure," I said.

Sue didn't respond but I took no offense. Our conversations had always been sparse, so I'd come to assume she didn't like to waste words. I knew enough about her to know she was an internal medicine physician with a sense of humor. At one JOI get-together, she played the part of a mad doctor, dispensing yellow fever inoculations for those who still needed them while wearing a whirly cap and smock splattered with fake blood. I knew she'd noticed a lump on the edge of her right breast almost five years ago while on a mid-summer canoe trip with her two daughters in Canada. Not wanting to ruin the rest of the summer—her family had several more trips planned—she kept quiet until her routine mammogram in early September. After that she was caught in a cascade of medical appointments and breast cancer treatments. Two years later she went on a snowshoe hike up Mount Marcy, at 5,344 feet the highest peak in the Adirondacks. She had never been on Mount Marcy, let alone in snowshoes, and since her diagnosis hadn't spent a significant amount of time being active indoors or out. Though slow and exhausted most of the climb, she made it to the summit. Sue had moxie.

Eventually I learned Linda Number One's story as well.

Advised to get a lumpectomy for suspicious tissue in her right breast, she had protested. She wanted a double mastectomy instead. There was no reason, medically speaking, for a double mastectomy, but she'd already had two lumpectomies for what turned out to be non-cancerous tissue and she wanted to end the cycle. She had moxie too. After surgery, the pathology report not only showed pre-cancerous cells in her right breast, but tissue in her left breast—which had had no discernible problems—had already developed into cancer.

The three of us appreciate each other's company, even when we don't talk.

Like now on the mountain.

I wouldn't be able to hold a conversation if I tried. Even though I've doublechecked my gear and triple checked my pack's fit—snug, but not too tight—I can't shake my nerves. I wipe away more sweat.

Can I really do this climb? The question is moot, clearly. I'm already in Africa, already at the base of Mount Kilimanjaro, already putting one foot in front of the other. There is nowhere to go, at least for now, but up.

Still, I can't stop the second-guessing. My pack, weighing less than it did during training, inexplicably has become too heavy. I give it a quick hoist and search for the self-confidence that accompanied me a short time ago at the start of the trail, now muddy and slippery in spots. I take out my trekking poles, surprised to be needing them this early on.

I talk to Bill. *I'm not going to ask you to help get me to the top. Just help keep me safe.*

The line of hikers compresses and expands like an accordion as the day wears on. We walk, and walk, and walk some more. Fatigue sets in, even along the flatter stretches. Still we walk. Slowly, slowly.

The porters breeze by in roomy clothing and shoes with broken laces, saddled with backpacks, tables, chairs, tents, luggage, food, and other supplies. They have the right of way. We know they're coming because the call moves like dominoes from one hiker to another from the back of the line to the front. "Porter on the left!" or "Porter on the right!"—signaling us to move to the opposite side of the trail as quickly as possible. Rick explains that those who've worked with Yusuf the longest have the best shoes. Most pairs, some with flapping soles, are oversized donations from previous climbers. I look down at my own shoes. On a training hike, when I saw that Sue and Linda Number One had the same tan Asolo boots with orange trim, I went straight to the store to buy a pair—not strictly to be a copycat, but because mine were seven years old and I thought theirs were cute. I justified the hefty price tag by telling myself I had become a serious hiker, and serious hikers needed serious boots.

Even in their castoff shoes, the porters will arrive at camp long before we do. They could walk up the entire mountain in a day if they wanted—and they often do to transport last-minute necessities from the trailhead to base camp on summit night. It's hard to process that level of physical fitness. "Jambo," some of them say as they pass. Occasionally we get the slang "Mambo." The metal cookware they're hauling clangs with each step, a rhythmic chime that grows hushed in the distance.

No one keeps official statistics on the number of porters who die on Kilimanjaro, but word has it there are several fatalities each year from hypothermia. Porters carry such heavy loads already, they can't carry baggage with dry clothes for themselves.

"These guys need better boots," says a hiker named Kevin, walking behind me. "But they look happy to be here."

Kevin is a self-deprecating radiation oncologist who signed up for the trip after reading an article about Journeys of Inspiration in the *Democrat and Chronicle*. He's probably in his 50s. We've chatted only briefly on our training hikes, but I remember that before medical school he knew a doctor who always talked about some famous radiation oncologist who climbed Mount Kilimanjaro. When Kevin read the article, he was inspired to do the same.

Kevin is right. Most porters don't have access to safe water and sanitation at home, but they do look happy. This is a hard job, but it's a good job in this part of the world.

"Hydrate!" Rick's voice thunders from behind.

We all move to the side of the trail to take a break and do as Rick says. Hopefully, more water will keep at bay the headache I feel coming on. The dull pangs could be from being parched since I've forgotten, I now realize, about the "clear and copious pee" rule of thumb. Or the headache may be the start of altitude sickness. We're climbing more than 2,000 feet today, putting us at over 8,500 feet above sea level—the altitude when acute mountain sickness, the milder form of altitude sickness, usually kicks in. I forgot to take Diamox as planned yesterday. I'll have to remember when we get to camp.

My throat is so dry, the first swigs of water go down hard.

While we're stopped, I should probably reapply sunscreen. I pull out my tube as Linda Number Two—the younger Linda—pulls a notebook from her pack. A middle school science teacher, she will be diligently recording notes for her students, one of whom donated three dollars toward the climb in honor of his mother who died of cancer. Linda Number Two is using a monitor to track her heart rate and rhythm; a handheld anemometer to measure dew point, wind speed, and temperature; and a pulse oximeter to measure blood oxygen levels and show the effects of altitude on muscle tissue. Another breast cancer survivor, she is here with her husband, Paul, whose video camera is as much a part of his climbing equipment as his pack. Less than a month after learning about the Kilimanjaro trip from Rick, Paul threw his wife an American Cancer Society fundraising party at a winery to celebrate her tenth year as a survivor. Linda Number One was there. They live in the same town and have been friends a long

Chapter 9

time. Linda Number Two hugged Linda Number One and said, "I know what our next adventure should be!" Linda Number One replied, "Yeah, I've got an idea too!" They soon understood they were talking about the same trip.

Back on the trail after our water break, my boots make muffled, dull thumps on the damp path. Aside from that, the quiet is arresting. The mountain is flecked with pines, woody vines, and elephant trails. Those trails are much wider than ours, with ruts so deep they look bulldozed. I'm just glad we get to have our own route.

While no Ireland, this place has some pretty impressive shades of green—emerald, shamrock, pear. Spanish moss drapes trees with gnarly branches. "I can't believe this scenery," I say to no one in particular as I pull my camera out of the case strapped strategically to the outside of my pack for easy access. I take a picture of the pristine rainforest. It is thicker than any forest I have ever been in.

All around us, Yusuf points out, are the curled tips of tree ferns called monkey tails.

"And here are pink, seahorse-shaped Impatiens Kilimanjari—also known as the elephant trunk flower—found nowhere else on earth but on the jungle floor of Kilimanjaro," he says.

Why only here? The world can be so mysterious.

Chapter 10

I left the Church after Michelle's biological father and I married. Since he'd wed previously in a Catholic ceremony yet never received an annulment, we weren't allowed, according to Catholic rule, to have a Catholic ceremony—and that infuriated me. I was long tired of the Church's strict rules anyway, such as having to confess on Saturday in order to earn Communion on Sunday. Of course I felt like I was letting down my devout mother. But she never admonished me or made me feel like I wasn't fit to make my own decisions, although I'm fairly certain she prayed for my soul every chance she got.

Without a church service to attend, weekends felt longer and offered more time for chores, which was nice. Even so, weekly Mass had been a dependable part of my life since I could remember and I missed parts of it terribly. I doubled up on my prayers to compensate. I may not have had a faith community, but I still had my faith. It was the oldest thing I owned. My mother had said grace and nighttime prayers with me since before I could understand language. And every Sunday she'd taken me, my two sisters, and my brother to the church around the block. That was back when services were in Latin. When I was too young to know what was going on, there was still something about the order of the Mass that made me feel like I was part of something special. I felt like I belonged there. I always knew when to sit or stand or kneel. I knew it was a place to be silent, a place to dip my short fingers in holy water, bless myself, and be seated in the same spot in the same pew near the back of the nave.

When Michelle was a baby and then a toddler, I often took her with me on a weekday to Sacred Heart Cathedral, the Mother Church of the Diocese of Rochester, where the walls were mostly plaster but painted to look like granite. The ornate cathedral was so much different from the long, narrow, simple church I grew up in. More than a hundred religious images garnished murals, columns, and the ceiling. To the right of the main altar was a wrought-iron stairway leading to an enormous pulpit; to the left, a decorative wood canopy hovered over the bishop's throne. Alcoves on either side held statues of the Virgin Mary and Saint Joseph, and in the center towered a gilded statue of Jesus, a visible heart bursting with light on his chest. I'd choose a dark oak pew in the back of the sanctuary and whisper prayers beneath dim lanterns—all while feeling guilty I wasn't raising Michelle in the Church.

Decades later, days before my brother passed away, his wife called me from beside his hospital bed to say she was vowing to return to Catholicism, which she had left years earlier. Maybe if she felt closer to God in a physical way, she would feel closer to Jerry once he passed on. Whatever her reason, her decision somehow shifted something in me and I resolved—out loud, while on the phone with her—to do the same.

At Saint Bridget's, the only Catholic church in Bloomfield, Sister Diane took me by the hand and, week after week, said, "This is the kinder, gentler Catholic Church." She was somewhat right. At least I was allowed to talk with the priest without a screen between us. When I went for my first confession at age seven, I was so scared I couldn't bring myself to make a sound. I just sat there in the dark, intimidated by the intricately carved confessional and the hidden priest in the neighboring compartment. My mother knew the priest well—she even cleaned his house every week—but that was no comfort to me. I hung my head and cried. Hearing me, the priest opened his door, then mine. "Come over with me," he said. I followed, keeping my head down and my eyes on the way his robe gently swept the floor. We went to his side of the confessional. He sat down and patted his legs. "Just so you know," he cautioned, "you can't do this every time." I nodded and sat on his lap. What a privilege to be in that cabinet, something I didn't think any of my friends had done. Through sniffles I told him what I'd rehearsed— that I had lied three times to my mother and yelled three times at my brother. The priest said, "Don't lie to your mother and don't yell at your brother." The next morning I carefully put on the frilly white dress, white patent leather shoes, and white veil my grandmother had bought for my First Communion, which I'd missed two weeks earlier because of the chicken pox. A fervent lifelong Catholic, Grandma Bea said the rosary every day and kept a basket of devotionals and prayer cards next to the velvety, overstuffed armchair in her apartment off the living room in our house. My mother, looking more formal than usual for my big day, wore a dress with lace around the collar and short heels. She worked on calming my nerves—the whole congregation would be watching me, after all—as she brushed my hair. I took a breath with every stroke. When we got to the church we sat in the front row instead of near the back like usual. It felt so different being that close to the altar, almost like we were being given easier access to the Holy Spirit. When it came time for Communion, I was grateful I'd had the chicken pox because I got to stand in front of everybody all by myself and receive the Body of Christ before anyone else.

A kinder, gentler Church aside, I'd been forbidden from taking Communion on Sundays until Bill and I married in a Catholic ceremony. Though baptized, Bill had never gone to church as a child or adult, and while happy to help navigate my own logistical hoops with the Church, he showed no interest in attending despite my sporadic invitations. That changed two years before the accident when a man from Saint Bridget's died of a heart attack. At a church event I'd dragged him to months earlier, Bill had gotten into a serious conversation with the man, who had extended an invitation of his own. Once the man was gone, that was that. Bill went through a process called the Rite of Christian Initiation of Adults required for Catholic converts. We started saying the rosary and praying before meals together. Bill volunteered for church activities and served as an usher on Sundays. He knelt at night to say his prayers, something I had never done. It was as if he were trying to make up for lost time.

Bill was in the middle of a religious retreat when he died. I found the spiral-bound journal he was using for the retreat after the accident when I was going through his desk, which felt equal parts intrusive and sentimental. I couldn't open the journal right away. Instead I ran my hand slowly down its spine and let my fingers bounce along the metal coils. As long as I didn't know what he'd written, Bill had something new to share with me. Eventually I peeked. The inside was filled with questions and revelations about faith and sin. "How would Jesus be received today as a person?" he wrote. "'Looked at the cat & thought about the cat not being able to commit sin." On the last couple pages, there were several iterations of what looked like a prayer adapted from Psalm 25. The last ended with, "Lord, show me and teach me your ways. Direct me to your truth, for you are God, my Savior."

I closed my eyes. The way the prayer had evolved with each version was so much like him. Scrupulously thoughtful, he'd work a situation until it didn't recognize itself—a trait that could try my patience. Had he been completely satisfied with this last one?

Chapter 11

The thick roots of a fallen tree divide the Lemosho trail as we approach a particularly steep ascent. Steps become slower and more calculated.

"Porter on the left!" several call from behind. I move to the right. A young man, in blue shorts over black long johns and a shirt with only the last button fastened, strolls by with a huge white sack balanced on his shoulders. His head is bent, his hands hang at his side. I've been sweating in shorts over bare legs. How can he stand the heat with all those clothes and all that weight? Not long after, we pass a small, skinny porter slouched on the ground as if he can't move another foot. He can't be more than 14. I've never seen him before and there has to be more than 100 pounds of gear at his side, so he must belong to another outfit. He looks sick enough to be in bed. Though I have faith that God has a plan for this world, sometimes it feels like a crapshoot why I had the good fortune to be born to middle-class parents in an economically stable country, while this boy is here in this position.

I tilt my face to the sky. *Please take care of this child.*

That six dollars a day is standard pay for mountain work is repulsive. It makes more sense now why the men at Londorosi Gate are so desperate for Yusuf to hire them—especially when they can only do this type of work six months of the year during the so-called climbing season. I can't imagine what this sick boy's life must be like. The only thing I can do is keep praying for him.

Soon we pass a nest of leaves bigger than a basketball.

"A spider nest," Mohammed the rear guide says, telling us the spiders are about the size of a deck of cards.

I hope our tents zip up all the way.

After four hours on the trail and the occasional rain shower—rain poncho on, rain poncho off—we reach Mti Mkubwa Camp, otherwise known as Big Tree Camp, at 9,152 feet. We hiked about as long as it takes to watch two movies, but this felt much, much longer. Every itinerary I'd seen online for the Lemosho Trail estimated today's hike at between two and three hours, so why did it take us four? Maybe it's hard to make good time with a group our size.

We're not the only group camping here tonight, but there's plenty of room and it's easy enough to find our blue tents packed tightly together. At each door are two green plastic sacks secured with rope. Our duffels are inside them.

"Go find your bags and get settled," Rick says. "There's hot tea, cocoa, popcorn, and chocolates in the food tent. The porters will be coming around soon with water for you to wash up."

Chocolates? I think of Grandma Bea, who would retrieve a box of Russell Stover chocolates from her underwear drawer so we could snack on them in secret while watching "Gunsmoke." Maybe my sense of adventure started there. Maybe my thriftiness did too—she also kept a nickel taped to the underside of a plastic Jesus on her dresser, convinced it would guarantee financial stability.

I search through the sacks, identifiable by our names written in black marker, while a small crowd gathers at a nearby tree to gawk at black-and-white Colobus monkeys swinging in the branches. They look like skunks with their long, bushy tails. I have an important task at hand, so that spectacle can wait. The universal piece of advice I'd gleaned from numerous high-altitude hiking experts was to keep the tent exceedingly organized. With increasing challenges at increasing altitudes, an orderly layout will be critical. Those experts spoke my language. Just five months ago I ordered all new kitchen appliances, after my refrigerator and dishwasher conked out in unison, because I wouldn't have been able to tolerate a mismatched stove. If Bill had been around he would have tried to make the repairs. And if we were on this mountain together he'd blow up my air mattress, set out my sleeping bag, and go to breakfast early every morning to have a cup of coffee waiting for my arrival.

This is all on me now.

At first Rick's five-page packing list had made my head reel. Broken down into 17 categories, the list told us which brands made for better-wicking shirts and gave the recommended size—in cubic inches—of the hip belts on our day packs. How to dress on summit night had multiple options. Choices included long johns and ski pants; or long johns, hiking pants, and rain pants; or long johns, fleece pants, and rain pants. So many decisions to make. "Remember," Rick had written, "you are moving too slowly to generate any body heat. It is like standing in line at the chair lift on a cold day." Back home I'd dug through bins of equipment I could still see Bill organizing and was thankful he was fastidious with handwritten labels. "Toiletries." "Sleeping items." "Compression sacks." A joke in our house was that God himself may have a hard time finding something, but Bill would know where it was. The packing would've gone faster if I hadn't spent so much time tracing over his scratchy handwriting. At the same time, I made preparations even more exhaustive by cleaning the tread of my hiking boots with a nail brush. I wanted everything in tip-top shape.

With bag in hand, I enter my tent and get to work immediately. It's satisfying to deftly carry out details I've spun around in my mind for months. Streamlining is a rush. Maybe that comes from my childhood, when what we had for dinner depended on the day of the week. Saturday, hot dogs or hamburgers. Sunday, pot roast or chicken with biscuits. Thursday, spaghetti. Friday, fish. I inflate my sleeping pad to put atop the sleeping mat provided with the tent, then unroll my sleeping bag, set out the clothes I'll need to wear next, and find a sensible spot for each hand-labeled ditty bag. Headlamp and lip balm go in one of the tent's side pockets. An old pair of low-cut hiking shoes that I can slide on like slippers get positioned within easy reach of my pillow in case of a middle-of-the-night need to use the bathroom.

I wonder where Sue is—not that she will need a lot of time to set up. From our two nights at the Springlands Hotel, I've learned she smooshes belongings in her bag willy-nilly, then wonders aloud where something is when she needs it. She may not even unpack at all. When Sue found out Jim and I were dating, she said, "You don't have to be my tentmate, you know." I knew what she was implying—that I could ask Jim to switch routes and she could pair up with someone else. But I would never bail on a commitment. Sharing a tent with Jim would've made things easier, no question, but I didn't want to make things easier. What mattered more was proving to myself that I could do this on my own, with a community by my side and without a man in my tent.

The porters come around with tubs of hot water as promised just as I pull a jar of face cream from the designated cosmetics bag. Perfect timing.

I'm lost in the gratifying massage of my nubby washcloth when Sue ducks into the tent.

"What are you doing?" She sounds incredulous.

I laugh. "I don't want to dry up into a little prune."

Sue tosses her bulging bag to the side and is out again lickety-split. How does she function that way? Even if my bathroom sink has been swapped for a scratched-up plastic tub, I need to stick to my routine. I hang the washcloth on a tent cord to dry and decide to use some of my alone time before dinner to jot a note in my journal: *Bill, you know Jim is taking such good care of me. He asked me yesterday if I thought I'd be okay. I didn't know, but I do know I'm with people who love me and will help me through this.*

I feel a chill. The temperature has fallen into the high 40s, and is still dropping quickly, so I change into long underwear, wind pants, a long-sleeve polypropylene shirt, and a light jacket. I slip on the low-cut shoes, pop a headlamp into my pocket, and head to the food tent for tea before dinner. A porter nicknamed "The Doctor" is setting up the toilet tent. His job is to carry the tent up the mountain and make sure it stays in working order. He will see to it that the black bucket with the liner and toilet seat stays clean, and that there's always toilet paper in the net pocket. We've been told to use the toilet tent only for serious business.

The roof of the food tent is so slanted, it's almost impossible to stand up straight or even sit upright. We all hunch on wobbly metal folding chairs around two long tables pushed together. Happy I'm not claustrophobic, I dig into canisters filled with salty popcorn and cookies, let the tea settle on my tongue, and listen to other people talk.

"You okay?" Linda Number One asks from across the table. Her question surprises me. I didn't realize my expression may be implying otherwise.

I nod. "I really miss Bill. He would've loved it here."

Dinner is a veritable banquet of fried fish, potatoes, soup, sauerkraut, and mixed vegetables. Flickering candles are propped inside split-open baked potatoes for support. Too bad the instant coffee is so awful. I admit to being a coffee snob. Back home I regularly drink up to four cups of ground coffee every day—black in the morning, with cream in the afternoon, a cappuccino or latte thrown into the mix on occasion—and often enjoy a cup on my way to the nearest Starbucks. I once refused to buy a minivan because a cup holder for my coffee wasn't next to the driver's seat. Bill used to laugh when, out of habit, I'd reach for a cup even when one wasn't there.

Most of our group combines the instant coffee with Milo, a malty, chocolate-flavored drink mix. Instead I fill my glass mug with hot tea and powdered milk and try to imagine I'm holding a chai latte, warm and sweet and mild. I tap my finger against the glass. Wouldn't plastic mugs be easier for the porters to carry up the mountain? It would be interesting to know how they divide the labor—whether by weight or bulk or without any deliberation at all.

Famished, I feast as quickly as I can, too focused on my food to pay much attention to Rick talking about our lead guide. But when I hear that Mohammed is 55, I look up from my plate. I thought he was at least a decade younger. Rick says that Mohammed has climbed to the top of Kilimanjaro more than 60 times and that he rents a two-room house with his wife, three-year-old son, and two other families for 30 dollars a month.

Maybe we value our independence too much in the West. As a culture we don't have to share our space or barter the way people do here, and there's a cost to that. We forget we need each other.

After we're served bananas for dessert, Rick reads abridged emails from our supporters back home. Hooray for satellite phones. When I hear Katie's "You can do it, Grammee!" and Michelle's "Sending love and prayers to you, Mom," the lump in my throat is so big I'm glad there's no more food on my plate to swallow. When Rick is done, he asks if we'll consider helping out Saidi who is recovering well from the malaria. Saidi recently earned the third-highest score in Tanzania on a math exam and wants to become an accountant. He won a university scholarship but needs to make up the difference in tuition. It breaks my heart that Africans have to struggle so hard to earn what we could earn much more easily—and still they smile and laugh way more often. From the media, it seems to people in Africa that most of us in the United States are wealthy and happy. I heard Yusuf say once that people in his country don't understand how we can have homelessness or jails.

Yusuf sticks his head into the tent and flashes his dimples. He's wearing a red knit cap ringed with stars. "So for tomorrow, you will need to carry three liters of water, a light jacket, and sunscreen."

I patiently listen to the rest of his instructions, though I'm caught off guard midway through by how worn out I am. As soon as the briefing is over, I want nothing more than to retreat to my tent. I pass on watching the Colobus monkeys swing in the trees as darkness falls. The stars overhead are almost ostentatious in their denseness. The temperature is close to 25 degrees colder now so I hug myself to keep warm.

"Lala salama," a few hikers call out as I walk away.

"Sleep well," I call back.

Inside the tent, I tuck my hat, balaclava, and extra gloves into the tent pouch closest to my sleeping bag in case I need them before sunrise, and down my first dose of Diamox. I fall asleep quickly but am soon reaching for the shoes by my head. Diamox wreaks havoc on the bladder. Flashlight in hand, frustrated that a drug made for use in the outdoors is a diuretic, I begin to unzip the tent. A monkey calls out overhead. Its deep, guttural rattle echoes over the hills and is the most horrendous sound I have ever heard. How can an animal even make a noise like that? What if there are more on the ground?

I zip the tent back up. My bladder will have to wait. Morning will be here soon enough.

Chapter 12

I kept my fingers loosely wrapped around the straps of my backpack.

Just across the Delaware River from New Jersey, I was hiking solo inside the Delaware Water Gap National Recreation Area in the Pocono Mountains of northeast Pennsylvania.

Bill and I had read about this place in Bill Bryson's *A Walk in the Woods: Rediscovering America on the Appalachian Trail.* That book had spun hours of discussion about us someday being on the longest hiking-only footpath in the world—if only parts of it—once we both retired.

I'd driven down here in my car instead of the new truck and camper Bill and I had planned on buying had things been different. It was my second summer without him.

The hike was pleasant enough at first. I passed the time listening to birdsong and identifying shapes in fallen tree limbs—an anchor, a playground slide, the arched back of a dragon submerged in water—until the scrape of a bush branch against my bare leg sent my mind reeling. It triggered memories from my hikes with Bill that had me cataloging sensory details as if thumbing through a deck of cards: the eerie call of a loon and the rustle of chipmunks, padding over earth that gave way like worn floor planks underfoot, hiking through spiderwebs and over upturned trees with knotted roots that looked like they understood the mysteries of the universe.

I heard what I could imagine were Bill's footsteps behind me, but I knew better.

The memories kept me occupied long enough to lose my place on the trail. I searched from tree to tree for a trail marker but my eyes landed only on rough bark. My pace became slow, doubtful. I felt like an easy target—for what kind of predator I didn't know. At a training session for volunteers at Serenity House, the home for the dying where I'd been spending more time, our first task was to make a list of what was most important to us. I started with family, friends, mobility. The next task was to cross off each item on the list, one by one, relinquishing what we valued most. That's what it's going to be like in the end for all of us, we were told—just ourselves, complete vulnerability.

There was nothing to do but choose a direction and keep walking.

I'd been giving more serious thought to what it meant to be alone. People frequently asked whether I had plans to relocate to North Carolina to be closer to Michelle. One woman told me, "If I didn't work and my daughter was my only family, I'd move south in a heartbeat." She said that as if retirement should prompt me to pack up my things and leave my life in Bloomfield behind. As if I didn't have my priorities straight. The woman's words stung at first and made me briefly wonder whether I was wrong to want to stay put. But I knew where I belonged. I liked that Bloomfield was the kind of place where everyone knew everyone else, for better or worse—that employees at the family-run grocery store knew my first name, that my pizza got delivered to my house by the pizzeria owner, that I could spend a breezy half hour at the post office moving from one conversation to another with other customers I've known for years, even decades. I had come from Canisteo, a small

Upstate New York village where memories were even more homespun. The entire town had been like one big neighborhood. The man who delivered eggs every week walked in our side door and found his payment in an envelope on the dining room table. The man who collected our weekly insurance payment sometimes would sit at that same table, after letting himself in, waiting for my mother to come home so they could visit for a while. Even potato chips were hand-delivered to our house every two weeks. I bet that woman who thought I should move south didn't think about the possibility of Michelle someday deciding to take a job offer in another state. What would I do then, chase my child around the country?

I walked and walked until the dirt trail turned to grass by a stream. Though unquestionably not anywhere near the right path anymore—or any path—I was so struck by the soothing sounds of the water, I wanted to stay. I pulled a forgettable novel out of my pack. I'd always told myself that once I was off the clock for good, I would read for pleasure, not just to learn something, and these days books had as much a place in my pack as sunscreen and bug spray. I sat against a log and read for what felt like hours. After standing back up, I made fun of myself for getting lost both on my walk and on the page.

It took two attempts, but I was able to find a trail that remained a trail. Again in the shelter of the woods, I thought I heard Bill's heavy gait on the dirt. *Thump, thump.* I started imagining him pointing out the ravine dominated by mature hemlock and mixed hardwood trees. I could see the wonder on his face. The memories tried to hang me up, but the fantasies pushed me on. Wasn't a phantom husband better than no husband at all?

"This is what we wanted to do," I said aloud.

Chapter 13

"Maji moto!" The porters are calling our attention to the half-full basins of water they're setting in front of each tent. Though their calls translate literally to "hot water," the temperature is more tepid than hot. The basins are for washing our faces and brushing our teeth.

The porters have been busy this morning. They woke us up a few minutes ago by delivering tea, presented on a tray with one tin spoon for measuring raw cane sugar and another for stirring. It feels decadent to be sipping hand-delivered tea in a tent, so I'm hoping my bulging bladder holds out a while longer.

I'm more tired than usual first thing in the morning. Not yet fully awake, I languidly push my water bottle and hydration pack onto the mat outside the tent. The porters will fill them with stream water they've collected and boiled.

It had been a long night between the coughing, snoring, monkey calls, and steady rhythm of tent zippers. I suppose a lot of us needed the bathroom before dawn. I know from Rick's stories that Yusuf would've awakened an hour before everyone else to check on those he heard coughing through the night. He always wakes without an alarm. Even when he's home, in a town about a

20-minute walk from Moshi, he rises early—earlier than his wife and three children—to go running. The pace he must keep on the mountain is much too slow for him to consider it a worthwhile form of exercise. Right now, for myself, getting dressed for the day could qualify as a decent workout.

Sue rolls over in her sleeping bag. Hearing other hikers outside the tent, I throw back the rest of my tea, popping iron pills, vitamins, and Advil in the process. The iron pills are a holdover from my second round of chemotherapy, which zapped my energy to such a degree that no food regimen—not even one packed with iron-rich meals culled from my nutrition books—could compete. Next, I take the Diamox and mefloquine, the malaria preventative.

Desperately needing to go to the bathroom now, I pack most everything I'll need for the day in minutes and slather on a base layer of sunscreen. After slipping a baggie for clean toilet paper in my right pocket and a baggie for used toilet paper in my left pocket, I pull a first-aid kit from my duffel and transfer a handful of Advil from a jumbo-sized bottle to a small container clipped to the outside of my pack. Between my own thumping head and fielding several requests for pills yesterday from hikers with headaches, the container already needs a refill. To the pouch on my hip storing lip balm and hand sanitizer, I add a sleeve of peanut-butter-and-cheese crackers that have become my preferred staple food when hiking. I tie my buff around my head. The stretchy tube of fabric can be worn in multiple ways, and when it gets colder up the mountain, I'll move it down around my neck.

Then my whirlwind preparations come to a halt.

I feel nauseated. Is it possible to have acute mountain sickness this soon? I bolt out of the tent toward the woods, passing Rick, Linda Number Two, and Paul, who's dipping his toothbrush in his scuffed water basin.

"Pretty sure I'm going to be the winner!" I shout, alluding to the bets made back at the hotel about who would be the first to throw up on the mountain. Not the bragging rights I typically strive to earn.

I barf at the base of a tree.

I can't believe I'm crouched here, barely beyond the start of the trail. Forget about my bladder. If this is how my body is responding now, how will it react tomorrow? What about five days from now when we attempt to summit? Rick will send me back if I develop severe altitude sickness. What about the vision I've been cultivating over these last 14 months?

Rick is used to this, I tell myself. He has seen his fair share of vomit and is well-versed in helping people push on through pounding headaches, diarrhea, dizziness, and hallucinations. Sometimes he's the ailing one. In Nepal he kneeled in yak dung while retching under a cold, twinkling sky. In Costa Rica, barely able to stand after 24 hours of consecutive vomiting, he stopped the bus he was on every few minutes to heave on the side of the road. He has had the honor, in fact, of vomiting on all seven continents. Reaching Kilimanjaro's Uhuru Peak may be uneventful for him on one trip, and on the next it's all he can do to stay on his feet. "You just never can tell what the altitude will do," he had warned us before we left New York.

It's not like I came here unprepared. I'd gotten my tetanus, Hepatitis A, influenza, and yellow fever vaccinations. I'd packed lots of pills, even those to prevent typhoid fever, that I bought from Kevin, the oncologist, during a JOI fundraiser. He sold them to us at cost from the back room of a cavernous concert hall, making the transaction feel like a different sort of drug deal. I'd also been tapped as a frequent contributor to local media, which gave me the chance to talk about Bill and how much this climb means to me. Newspaper headlines included "A Tall Challenge" and "Climbing Project is also Life Support." I'd been quoted in the *Daily Messenger*, saying, "I don't know if that mountain's going to hold all those emotions." I'd even gotten a fresh haircut, the same style I've had since I was 12, short enough to barely graze my ears and with

Chapter 13

wisps for bangs. But this—folded over in the dirt, wiping my mouth with the hem of my shirt—wasn't in the plans. I'm not the oldest here but I'm certainly not the youngest. Maybe this is too much for me. Another wave of nausea and my fingers grip the ground. What was I thinking?

"This is not altitude sickness."

I say it so it will be true.

"This could be altitude sickness."

I say it because I don't know what the hell I'm talking about.

I hear murmuring and I'm guessing it's about me.

Should I turn back and leave this formidable pilgrimage to the others? It wouldn't be the first time.

Chapter 14

Hikers from three counties had joined Journeys of Inspiration by the time the group met up at Grimes Glen, a deep gorge cutting through layers of shale and limestone in the village of Naples. Kilimanjaro was eight months away.

As he did before every training hike, Rick corralled everyone into a wide circle.

"Let's talk about what brings you guys out here," he said.

Jim, standing next to me, held up a finger, volunteering to go first. "The thing I love about hiking," he said, "is that you spend all day out there, you get really tired, you go back to your car and say, 'Why do I do this?' and the next day you wake up ready to do it again."

Everybody laughs.

That's how it had been with Bill. Even when we got lost on a trail for hours, after finding our way back to the car and a good night's sleep, one of us inevitably would ask, "Where do you want to go today?"

I turned toward Jim, who I still didn't know all that well. "I know exactly what you mean."

Chapter 14

After everyone had their turn, we took a short trail leading over a small bridge and through a creek toward a 60-foot waterfall. Some of the men scrambled past clumps of purple loosestrife, over moss-covered rocks and logs, and up the side of the gorge—hanging onto jutting tree limbs for support—to get to the top of the waterfall. I would've rather licked a toad. I waited on the flattest rock I could find, next to a woman who wasn't part of our group. We stared skyward as the men reached the crest, waved their arms, and hollered to us below.

"Is your husband up there?" the woman asked.

I felt sucker-punched. Fixing my gaze on the brink of the waterfall, I replied, "No. My husband passed away a couple years ago."

"I'm sorry. I shouldn't have asked."

"No problem." Of course it was a problem. "How would you know?"

I wished I were home. There were lots of other ways I could be preparing for this weeklong climb on the other side of the world. One of them was by reading—a solo activity without the threat of triggering questions. I'd been spending a lot of time on the couch with books about Kilimanjaro. I had even breezed through Ernest Hemingway's famous short story, *The Snows of Kilimanjaro*, though it mentions the mountain only briefly in two places, which was a letdown. A more practical read was a guide called *Climbing Mount Kilimanjaro*. The guide was so excessively thorough, it included a recommendation for women to coordinate the climb with their menstrual cycle. I no longer had to worry about that, but the detailed tips on training, equipment, and other preparations were insightful. In some respects I wished they weren't. The couple made the climb sound brutal. In the husband's day-by-day diary, he wrote that scaling the summit was "pure misery" and that his wife collapsed "dramatically" during her attempt. I tried to take the passages with a grain of salt. Just because they had that experience didn't mean I would. But I might. And the fact that the guide was written by a married couple only made the reality that I was gearing up for this climb on my own more conspicuous.

I closed my eyes, wanting nothing more than to get back to my car.

We were scheduled to go right after this to another gorge at Conklin Gully just outside Naples. As plans stood, we would eat lunch there before hiking along a series of waterfalls. I had no interest in eating or the scenery.

At least the men had started making their way back down. I fidgeted until they reached us.

On our way back to the parking lot, I could barely concentrate. I struggled to keep my footing on the flat ground. It was all I could do to avoid the white, fragile Indian pipe plants in the middle of the trail.

I prayed I didn't stumble and fall.

Jack and Jim, who had volunteered at the first JOI dinner to provide food on our training hikes, drove out first to set up for lunch. I followed close behind with the rest of the crew.

As soon as I pulled into the gravel lot and spotted the trailhead, I regretted pulling off the road. I considered turning around but another car, already behind me, prevented a discreet exit. Frustrated, I got out of my car, still trying to think of a way to leave without drawing attention. I didn't want to have to explain to strangers—because most of them still were strangers—why a peaceful hike on a gorgeous day made me sullen and weepy.

"Okay, everybody!" shouted Jim, pointing to a menu taped to the side of his car and to printed copies next to the food. I got the sense that, like me, he was a thorough planner. "Come make your sandwich and put it in your pack."

I had to admit the menu was impressive. Made-to-order turkey wraps with a variety of condiment choices, an assortment of fresh fruit and drinks, trail mix, and chocolate cupcakes with buttercream icing.

Chapter 14

"Hey Bonnie!" Rick summoned, waving me over to him. He nodded toward Jack and Jim. "Get a load of those guys over there. Think we should've brought them aprons?"

I forced a smile.

"We'll eat by the waterfall," he called out to the group.

I knew my stomach couldn't handle a bite of anything.

"Time to grab my gear," Rick said. "Be right back."

I concentrated on the sound of his boots grinding gravel as he walked to his car, and to the lively chatter of the hikers layering cold cuts. Kicking at the stones at my feet, I had no doubt I needed to go home.

I walked over to Rick's car. He was fiddling with his pack. When he looked at me, I crumbled.

"This is harder than I thought it would be," I said through tears. "You have to help get me out of here."

"Aw, Bonnie." He gave me a hug and, thankfully, requested no more information. "You got it."

I don't know how he did it, but Rick was able to get the car behind mine moved without anyone catching on to my drama. I waited under a looming sycamore tree, its shaggy bark in pieces around my feet. The hikers, all set with their sandwiches, started splashing up a culvert at the foot of the trail. Rick stayed behind and joined me under the tree. He'd be able to catch up to the others in no time.

"Are you going to be okay?" he asked.

"I just need some time by myself."

We stood in silence for a few moments, then hugged again. When I couldn't sob anymore, I pulled away.

"Are you sure you're going to be okay?" His eyes were wet.

My mind evoked images of Bill at the trailhead, his pack stuffed with our gear, his body turned toward me, waiting.

"Yes. I just can't be here right now."

I heard muffled sounds of laughter from the hikers.

"I'll catch you later," I said.

Rick walked away, then looked back to offer a consoling wave. I watched him until he disappeared around a bend.

Chapter 15

I'm pretty sure I'm all out of vomit.

Staring at the ground, I tell myself this isn't any form of altitude sickness and visualize making a sign of the cross.

Please give me strength, I pray. *Please give me strength.*

I'm a hell of a lot stronger than this. I'd beaten cancer twice. I had been a successful female engineer in a man's industry. I'd moved forward after Bill's sudden death. I'd signed up to climb Kilimanjaro.

I'm ON Kilimanjaro! I can do this!

I push myself up from the ground and brush dirt off my pants. Thank goodness no one stops me on my way to the toilet tent. I'm lucky I haven't had an accident by now.

Rick and Yusuf greet me as soon as I step back outside.

"We heard you were sick," Rick says. "Hope you're feeling better."

"Much better."

"Eat some millet porridge if you can."

I can think of worse things to try to keep down.

On the way back to my tent to finish getting ready for

breakfast, I hear a snippet of conversation between Paul and Linda Number Two.

"With all the snoring, farting, and zippers, I got about an hour's worth of sleep," he says.

"I slept maybe two or three hours," she says.

I have the tent to myself. Sue must have gone to the food tent. I pull Sister Dorothy's prayer from my daypack. The paper is soft now, having been folded and unfolded so many times. It begins:

> *Our Father, we place the Kili climbers*
> *in Your hands as they pursue this*
> *courageous, awesome journey*
> *of care, concern and hope.*

Sister Dorothy and I met when Bill and I were involved with the Catholic charity organization that brought East African families to Bloomfield. Later that same year I signed up for a nine-month spirituality retreat, and she was the retreat leader. Once, after we'd spent weeks on a series of readings about being remorseful for our transgressions, I asked, "When the heck are we going to be done with this sin stuff?" The complaint hadn't riled Sister Dorothy in the least. On the contrary, she skipped ahead to the next theme to appease me. It was a meditation on hell, but still, she tried. After Bill died, she called nearly every night to check in. Our friendship deepened, even more so after she canceled dinner with another nun to be with me on an exceptionally grueling night. "I appreciate you changing your plans," I said when she got to my house. She prolonged our embrace and said, "This is where I'm supposed to be tonight." She would say things like, "I don't know why God does what he does, but I believe there are hands that are taking care of us, there are eyes that are seeing us, there are feet that are walking with us. We have to be open to what God wants from us. We have a spirit, and spirits don't die." They were always things I believed already but needed to hear. Eventually she came over for supper every Sunday night. "Are you interested in a drink?" I'd ask, and she'd offer up one rhetorical response or another. "Is the Pope Catholic?" "Did the sun come up this morning?" "Am I still breathing?" One night, shortly after the whiskey was poured, she thrust a piece of paper into my hands.

The prayer continues:

Protect them and guide them up the heights,
Keep them safe from all dangers,
Dazzle them with the majestic beauty of creation,
Bless them as they place the names of friends, family
and loved ones in the hallowed place.
Celebrate with them as they reach their goal.
We pray for their safety as they return
a different way,
physically, emotionally and spiritually.
Help us to be ever grateful to them
for their heroic efforts for all people.
We ask these favors in Your Holy Name.
Amen.

I make a sign of the cross—for real this time.

Chapter 16

It was a sunny Saturday, and I despised sunny Saturdays. They pulled me back to the bright mornings I'd surprise Bill with bagels and cream cheese that we'd devour while planning our weekend. In a lousy mood by breakfast, I had blown off the JOI hike at Mendon Ponds Park and was tempted to break my commitment to help out that afternoon at the annual Genesee Valley Outdoor Expo. People went to the Expo to learn about a wide range of outdoor experiences, from hiking and paddling to learning map and compass skills. Our JOI group hiked together most weekends and was manning a booth there to recruit more climbers.

I didn't want to have to explain to anyone later why I'd missed both events, so I got in my car. The rays beat forcefully through the windshield as I followed signs along the park's winding main road to a parking lot jammed with Subarus and pick-up trucks. There wasn't an empty spot in sight. I was toying with the idea of returning home when I spied a spot in the grass large enough to fit my Honda Pilot.

The flashbacks started as soon as I got out of the car.

Hiking in the park with Bill beneath shagbark hickories.

Chapter 16

Watching the warbler migration with him in spring and letting chickadees eat sunflower seeds out of our hands in winter. Cross-country skiing with Bill and Michelle over wooden footbridges while searching for cardinals in the snow. Ice-skating with Michelle on one of the park's ponds while Bill went ice fishing on another. The scenes flickered in front of me until I was at the edge of the parking lot, at the top of a hill overlooking the Expo—a sea of tents and packed with people who seemed to have much lighter loads to carry.

I steadied myself and tried to muzzle the voice in my head telling me things were only going to get worse.

I walked down the hill and onto a path that snaked under cooling sycamores, white oaks, and eastern white pines. Dozens and dozens of tents held promotions for nature clubs and other outdoor recreational groups, or offered demonstrations on things like wilderness first aid, handmade fly reels, and practical ways to lighten your backpack. Canoes and kayaks dotted a pond close by.

When I got to the JOI booth, an unfamiliar woman from Pack, Paddle, Ski offered an enthusiastic welcome, as did Jim and Jack.

"I'm Bonnie," I said to the woman.

I gave a perfunctory wave to the guys.

"Hi," Jack said.

"I'm beginning to recognize you," Jim said.

I took my place behind a table covered with carefully fanned brochures about the Kilimanjaro trip. I did my best to smile and answer questions for interested strangers who lingered. One of them, an animated woman with short, fuzzy hair, introduced herself as Alison.

"I just read about you guys in the paper," Alison said. "I'm a marathon runner trying to get back into shape. I had treatment for breast cancer, and my hair is just starting to grow back."

"Can I touch it?" I was surprised by how easily the question tumbled out of my mouth. I wasn't sure whether to be mortified or pleased that I wanted to interact that closely with another human being.

"Sure." Alison bent her head forward. I reached over and smoothed my palm over her downy skull. When I had cancer, not wanting anyone to know I felt sick, I bought three wigs just so others would think I enjoyed switching things up as a blond, brunette, and redhead. I bought funky hats and big hoop earrings that I'd never been known for wearing, learned scarf-tying tricks and how best to apply makeup. I became adept at knowing when to flash a smile. All of it made other people feel good. When they thought I was doing well, their concerned expressions went slack. I learned how hard it was for people to hold painful emotions. That became even more evident after the accident.

I pulled back my hand from Alison's head. "It's so soft."

I laughed at myself, feeling the morning's tensions start to dissipate. Alison and I talked for a while before she jotted down her name, number, and e-mail so Rick could give her more details about the trip. I could see us training together, sharing the satisfaction over time of returning to what we loved, of celebrating a life undeterred by cancer. She made me feel, for the first time, the slightest sense of belonging to this fledgling group—and she wasn't even a part of it. I wished it were my job to follow up with her, but I still had a lot of learning to do about Kilimanjaro myself.

Looking at me, Jack pointed a thumb at Jim. "We're heading to the food tent. We got some coupons for free hot dogs."

I suddenly realized I was hungry. "Can I tag along?"

"Right this way," Jim said, ushering me to follow.

"Nice to meet you," I said to Alison, happy to be out of the fog in which we'd introduced ourselves.

The hot dog line was long and slow-moving, so I moved to the hamburger line. I had my meal in hand before the men had even placed their order. Pointing my plate toward the pond, I called over to them, "If you get your food in time and want to join me, I'll be sitting by that tree over there."

Chapter 16

The shade felt good now that the sun had moved directly overhead. I assessed the crowd, a bunch of outdoor enthusiasts eager to sign up for clubs, test drive canoes and kayaks, and make plans for the future.

The future.

My jaw slowed to an almost imperceptible grind. It became hard to swallow.

I couldn't picture my future.

What business did I have being at the Expo in the first place?

I stood up, threw away my unfinished meal, and returned to the booth. I wanted to run away but settled for deep-breathing exercises. Jack and Jim were eating their hot dogs at a picnic table behind the tent. I was annoyed they hadn't chosen to join me.

Maybe I would never really belong to this group.

I walked up to them and asked Jim, "Do you have any shirts with you?" Jim was in charge of selling polo shirts embroidered with the Journeys of Inspiration logo—a trail leading to Kilimanjaro and silhouetted by the sun. I thought they'd make nice parting gifts for two nuns who were moving from Saint Bridget's to another parish.

"In the back of my car," he said. "You want to take a look?"

"When you're done." I circled around to the front of the booth to wait, thankful no one was there to ask for information. Two minutes later, without the patience to wait any longer, I was back at the picnic table. "I'm leaving."

Jim wiped the crumbs from his hands. "Okay. Let's go to the car."

About halfway to the parking lot, I heard my name from behind. I turned to see a man who sometimes hiked with our group even though he wasn't going to Africa.

"Hey, we missed you today," he said. "I thought I'd see you on the trail."

I stopped.

I didn't respond at first, and when I did, my tone was curt. "I didn't make it. I'm not having a good day." I wheeled around and walked away, too drained to care about coming across as rude.

Jim was opening the hatch when I caught up. Inside were two boxes filled with neatly folded, brightly colored cotton shirts. I picked out two—one yellow, one lilac—and considered buying another for Katie.

"Do you have any kids'?" I asked.

"Yeah, a daughter in Las Vegas and a son in Boston."

I felt my stomach tighten. I didn't care about his children. "No, I mean kids' shirts." My voice was more disagreeable by the moment.

"Oh. Nope." His tone was soft. "Sorry."

I handed over the money, said a brusque "Thanks," and slogged up the rest of the hill to my car. The flashbacks returned, and I got lost driving out of the park I knew so well. All I could focus on was the sun searing the windows.

Chapter 17

"Mohammed is ready!" Yusuf's voice carries over the camp, signaling our lead guide's stance at the start of the trail. Brawny and tall, Mohammed wears a huge blue backpack and covers his hairless scalp with a colorful knit hat topped with a pom-pom.

"*Twende sasa!* That means, 'Let's go now!'" Yusuf says. Even when he's giving orders, he smiles.

I line up with the others, and for the first time notice the blue tents covered in raindrops from what must've been a light overnight shower.

It's already warmer than before breakfast.

The watery porridge in my belly is doing the trick. A few hikers who either saw or heard about my sprint to the woods offer sympathetic smiles. I wonder if they remember how I left them at Conklin Gully without saying goodbye. I'd emailed an apology afterward. I took my time crafting the message, wanting them to know I fully intended to be a team player on this trip—that I wasn't someone known for disappearing at a moment's notice. Questioning the validity of my pledge as I typed, I promised I wouldn't let them down and would be ready for Kilimanjaro.

Within days most everyone had replied to my email with thoughtful, compassionate remarks. Jim told me not to apologize. "Who knows what causes our emotions to do what they do?" he wrote.

Despite my rough start I feel up to walking although, as soon as we get going, my pace on the damp trail is slower than it was yesterday. We head through trees that give way to a valley carpeted with bushes and ferns as high as my hips. The air is noticeably thinner.

Yusuf catches up to us after about half an hour. He'd stayed behind to make sure the porters weren't having any problems packing up. Every day they will leave camp last and arrive at the next camp first.

In a short-sleeved shirt and still wearing the red knit cap, Yusuf promises to help pass the time with stories.

"I will start from the beginning," he says. "I come from the Pare tribe."

Born in a stick-and-mud hut in northeastern Tanzania's Pare Mountains, where the average income is less than 500 dollars a year, Yusuf grew up with two brothers and three sisters on a hillside about 45 miles east of Moshi. His family eventually built a cinderblock home with an outdoor kitchen, outhouse, and distant view of Lake Jipe on the border between Tanzania and Kenya. His father ran a small farm at the bottom of the hill and was rarely home. Yusuf did well in school and was accepted at a university to study medicine but his family, though proud, couldn't afford tuition. Instead he sold corn on the streets and juggled an assortment of odd jobs. One of them was translating movies in a bar in Mto wa Mbu, a community whose name means "River of Mosquitos." The bar was nothing more than a shack. Yusuf's English was poor but he could understand enough to explain in Swahili what was happening in the Billy Blanks and Jean-Claude Van Damme videos the bar's customers loved to watch. He'd lower the volume on the television set, powered by a generator because the bar had no electricity, and translate into a microphone. With Indian and Chinese movies he relied more heavily on his imagination. Ultimately he quit that job because it didn't pay well, and he was about to get paid even less. With electricity coming to the area, patrons would be buying their own television sets and wouldn't need him anymore. He thought about buying a popular tourist shop, but it was rainy season when he went to look at it and the place was under water. That's how Yusuf ended up on the mountain. He thought he could earn enough for medical school as a porter but soon realized his salary wouldn't come close to covering tuition. Mountain guides, on the other hand, made much more money, even more than doctors. He enrolled in night classes with the Tanzanian National Park Service to become a guide and bought instructional books to better his English. He loved the classes so much that he ditched the idea of medical school altogether. He preferred being in nature anyway. He spent one year as an assistant guide—the year he met Rick—and has been a main guide ever since.

Yusuf says that while he could see Kilimanjaro from the Pare Mountains, the thought never occurred to him—or to anyone in his tribe, for that matter—to climb it. The Pare people believe Uhuru Peak is connected with the afterlife—the reason they are required to face the mountain when they pray. Many from the region don't believe humans could even reach the top if they tried. Yusuf shrugs. "My father says no one can climb there because that is where God lives, and there is no way you can visit God until you die." The photos Yusuf has shown his father over the years—confirmation he has reached the summit of the Mountain of God, 200 times and counting—mean nothing. "He just says 'No, you and the government find a certain place you call the top of the mountain so you can get clients.' He asks my clients, 'Did you make it to the top?' and he is kind of laughing because he thinks, 'Your money is gone and you have not been anywhere.' I gave up trying to prove it."

Locals find it amusing that Americans spend so much money, travel so far, and suffer so much to climb a mountain the Africans look at every day.

"They say, 'Those wazungu,'" says Yusuf. "That is the Swahili word for white people."

Yusuf has seen how physical fitness, the weather, and altitude affect how high a person can climb. I have to imagine that growing up in a culture that believes in ancestral spirits, the power of the evil eye, and witchcraft, he also ascribes some of the odds to the whim of the mountain itself. To a question about whether we will reach the summit, I once heard him reply, "If the mother allows."

The trail narrows and tightens, and my stomach does the same. I don't want to hold up the line or stop listening to Yusuf's stories, but I need to slow down. I stop and wipe the sweat off my face. I don't want anyone wondering whether I still feel sick, so I do things I hope won't draw attention. I pause and crane my neck to look at the trees, so much taller and sinewy here, still dripping with shaggy moss. I reapply sunscreen. I take pictures of the stream in which, much farther below, the porters retrieved our water this morning.

Then back to it. When someone ahead announces we've made it to 9,400 feet, the line erupts with celebratory cheers.

Todd, one of the hikers I know the least about—only that he's a 30-something accountant with two kids and one on the way—walks up. "Hey, how are you feeling? You didn't look too good this morning."

I don't want to tell the truth. "Just fine."

"Bonnie," he says, "you're a badass."

I've never been called a badass before. It almost makes the morning's rocky start worth it.

"I don't know about that, but thank you!"

I point to the dappled sunlight filtering through overarching limbs, then to a smattering of mountains in the distance, a bulky ribbon of clouds behind them. One of the mountains is Mount

Meru, near the city of Arusha, looking like a squat triangle levitating in the otherwise bright blue sky.

"Can you believe all of this?"

Before Todd can say anything, we hear, "Porter on the left!"

We move to the side. One porter after another moves swiftly and silently past, their hands clasped in front of their bellies or adjusting the floppy sacks on their heads.

Then soon, 9,600 feet. Almost out of the tree line.

Rick spots Paul with his video camera and pretends he is too tired to go on. "The air...is...so thin...here," he jokes with a strained voice. Rick knows what's to come. Already the effort it takes to breathe is more noticeable by the hour. Is anyone else thinking what I'm thinking? That this is only the second day?

We file up and down a few puddled gullies and up and down some more before the trail slopes into a vast swath of heather. It gets chilly and starts to sprinkle. Just because we've left the rainforest doesn't mean we've left the rain, it seems. A few of us slide into thin raincoats.

Yusuf laughs. "No need. Like plants, we need the rain to make us grow."

Yusuf offers to help the more curious members of our group, myself included, get to know the land a little better. We learn to identify a type of fruit fly found only on the mountain, different species of trees, and the ferns he calls "the Grand Grandpa of the Rainforest" because they've been here so long.

"The forest knows much more than we do," he says. "There is a lot of diversity here."

Yusuf stands on his toes to get a better look at something behind me. "What is going on over there?" he asks.

A small group has gathered at the edge of the trail. We walk over. A chameleon balances on a thin branch, its bumpy skin a splotchy mess of yellow, black, and tan. There are so many unexpected visual treats here, including Shira Ridge directly ahead of us on the trail. The ridge is what's left of Kilimanjaro's first volcano and is the mountain's oldest and smallest summit.

We all continue on, our feet kicking up red dirt as we pass small wildflowers and shrubs, scrubby vegetation, a savanna of tall grasses. The air continues to cool. Alison, the woman I met at the Genesee Valley Outdoor Expo, moves with long, intent strides. Seems appropriate given that she'd introduced herself as a marathon runner. I was so happy when I found out she'd signed up for this trip. I feel responsible in some small way for her being here with us.

Once we pass Shira Ridge, the magnificent Kibo summit is before us, and I feel the magnitude of where I am.

So what if I threw up this morning? Look at what I get to see. I need to accept what happens next, whatever that may be, and enjoy being here in the meantime.

A white-necked raven flies overhead. The ring around the base of its skull is stark against feathers black as coal. Its call is a gurgling croak.

"Sounds like a warthog," Paul says as he films the bird.

I have to go to the bathroom. On yesterday's hike I never had to go to the bathroom—or, more accurately, to the side of the trail. I have no choice now. I've hiked enough to have peed off the trail more times than I can count, but usually in dense forests and without other people standing around. Some of the shrubs here are high enough for decent coverage, but it helps to conjure a memory of Kim, the woman carrying her father's ashes in her pack, to feel plucky enough to do what needs to be done. On one group training hike, we'd stopped at a waterfront restaurant to use its outdoor bathrooms. They were locked, so while someone went inside to request a key from the manager, Kim announced she couldn't wait any longer and relieved herself behind a row of boat docks pulled up in preparation for winter storage. I could never do that, I'd thought. I replay the image of her emerging from the docks—looking, appropriately, relieved—until my pants are zipped up once more. I jog back to the trail, still antsy. For no reason, it turns out. No one's even facing my direction.

We reach a part of the trail scarred by deep ruts that take careful maneuvering. I fiddle with my sunglasses, trying to adjust to the rampant dust caking my lenses and clothes. The packing list had said to bring only one or two pairs of pants, one T-shirt, and one long-sleeved shirt. I try not to think about how long it will be before I get them all into a washing machine—or that I have to wear them again and again until then. At least the buff tied behind my head keeps the dust out of my mouth. My fingers tingle from the Diamox, but we were warned that could happen so I'm not worried.

Stunted bushes replace the trees. We round a bend and I rest my hand on Linda Number One's arm.

"Am I having visions?" I ask.

I blink hard, trying to apply context to what's in front of me, to pull from some past frame of reference. Ahead of us, in a shallow valley, are tables with fabric tablecloths and cloth napkins. At each place setting is an avocado, orange, juice box, and toasted cheese, tomato, and green pepper sandwich.

"Let's find out," she says.

We move tentatively to the folding chairs. I grab hold of the back of one and give it a shake to verify its existence.

The porters must have done this for us. Such planning and care. This most definitely is no Greenland, where up to eight hours a day I had to carry a 40-pound pack loaded with clothes, the group's first-aid kit, and food—food that bore no resemblance to this feast.

My throat catches.

"Amazing," Kevin says. "They do everything here with so little. At home I need a gadget just to make anything the right way."

The meal is delicious and over way too quickly. When we're done, the porters pack up in a flash and recede into the distance along the trail. The white bags they carry make them look like sheep searching for a higher place to graze.

From this point on, the path is steeper. The wind is stronger too. I have to work harder to inhale. The temperature steadily drops and the clouds roll in, making it difficult to see much. I mark my movement by counting the number of bushes I brush past that have leaves like soft whiskers. The bushes remind me of low willows in the Arctic.

Finally, after six hours, we reach Shira 1 Camp at 11,480 feet. We are on the Shira Plateau now, the aftermath of an ancient volcanic eruption and one of the highest plateaus on earth. The clouds are so thick we can't see beyond the campsite. It's grassy and flat here, like a gigantic pasture, with a tiny stream and volcanic rocks bearded with lichen. Mountain rangers are based here in a ramshackle hut that stinks of propane.

The grit has settled into the cracks of my skin and stains the tissue I use to blow my nose. And I smell, making me impatient for the porters to come around with the water basins. I deal with the wait by changing out of my boots into more comfortable shoes—one of the most satisfying parts of any hike. I turn my damp socks inside out and string them on one of the tent cords to dry. One of the other hikers holds up the shirt she'd secured with bungee straps to the outside of her pack this morning. She had washed and rinsed the shirt last night, hoping it would finish drying during today's hike in the sun. That plan had technically worked—the shirt was dry—although the only clean spots after hiking in the dust were the crisscross marks of the bungee straps.

"Look at that!" The voice comes from somewhere behind me. I look over my shoulder.

The cloud cover is lifting up slowly from the ground like a stage curtain.

"Welcome to the show!" Rick says. "Your closest glimpse yet of the Kibo summit."

The glacier is taller than it ever was in my mind's eye. The

Chapter 17

sheer magnitude of what I'm here for isn't only a figment of my imagination anymore.

The porters, glistening with sweat in spite of the cold, are passing out basins of water.

"Jambo, jambo," they say.

"Jambo," I reply.

It's hard to picture the porters off the clock—able to be playful, not having to worry about catering to tourists with assumptions and expectations. I heard that once, after finding a package of condoms in the toilet tent, they blew them up and tossed them around like balloons.

After a spit bath—using the washcloth from yesterday, not the other one branded with a black "X" for private parts only—I feel as refreshed as possible without a proper soaking.

I wonder where Sue is and how she can stand the grime.

"There's hot chocolate for those who want it!"

I can't tell whose voice it is, but I'm grateful for the heads-up. Hot chocolate sounds lovely, although feeling spoiled from our lunch in the valley, I can't help wishing for the kind of spread we'd happened upon after an especially long training hike last fall. Finishing up a 17-mile walk around Conesus Lake, we reached a lakefront bait and grocery shop, its parking lot packed with motorcycles. Agreeing on the need for a pit stop, we went inside and stumbled upon a huge party. Apparently it was tradition for the store to hold an open house before closing for the season. There were free hors d'oeuvres, pitchers of Bloody Marys, bottles of Wild Turkey American Honey bourbon. We toasted our upcoming trip with plastic cups and talked with regulars captivated by our plan to climb Kilimanjaro—a buzz no amount of alcohol could match.

With my pack stowed away, I head to the food tent. It's about 25 degrees now and I can see my breath. Wailing winds pelt the exposed plateau. The camp sits in shadow with the sun's rays illuminating only the summit ahead, shining like a beacon. The door of the food tent flaps violently. Paul, making the rounds with his video camera, asks for a reflection on my experience so far.

"I'm not sure what I hoped for, but it's definitely more than I ever imagined."

Is Jim feeling the same way?

Chapter 18

Two months after the Outdoor Expo, I was slicing apples when I heard the high-pitched beep of the driveway alarm. The alarm was new, installed after tiring of sneaking to the window every time an animal tripped an outside light sensor. I'd never been nervous about that when Bill was in the house.

I set down the knife and walked to the side porch to greet Jim.

"Sorry I'm late," he said.

"No problem. I'm just hanging out."

"Your shirts are all right here." He opened his hatchback.

Jim had emailed the night before to say my order was ready. Seventeen embroidered JOI shirts for family and friends. The first ones I bought had been so well-received, I figured I should buy more. Jim had offered to deliver them because he was going to be in my area anyway. I thought it was a nice gesture. Wondering if he'd show up hungry given that he would be stopping by in the early afternoon, I had invited him to stay for lunch.

We'd been on several group hikes since the Expo and had gotten to know each other a little better. He was much more serious about hiking than I had ever been. He and Jack were the most experienced of the JOI bunch. Together they had reached the top of New Hampshire's Mount Washington, Tennessee's Clingman's Dome, and North Carolina's Mount Mitchell. They'd both worked as analytical chemists at Eastman Kodak Company and had become 46ers together—a designation for those who climb all 46 major peaks over 4,000 feet in the Adirondacks. They would start each year's climbs in May, typically lay low in June to avoid black fly season, then take steady trips through November, saving backcountry peaks for long weekends to bang out three or four at a time. They'd knock at least one more off the list in winter, usually in January. On our last hike together, Jim told me how Jack always knew they would keep doing big climbs after becoming 46ers, even if he himself had questions. "Questions?" I'd asked. "Cancer," he'd said. Most of the climbers had submitted a photograph and bio for me to post on the JOI website so I knew that Jim had had prostate cancer, but it had never come up in conversation. After mentioning his cancer—nonchalantly, while unwrapping a triple-decker peanut-butter-and-jelly sandwich—he continued. "I told Jack about my diagnosis and he said, 'You're going to have the surgery, you're going to be fixed, and that's all there is to it.' Four months later we climbed Longs Peak."

Longs Peak is part of the Rocky Mountain National Park in northern Colorado with a 14,259-foot summit. I thought about the highest altitude I'd reached up until then—a mere 3,800 feet, on top of Blue Mountain in the Adirondacks. I wondered, yet again, what business I had training for Kilimanjaro.

Jim set the box of shirts on my dining room table while I made our lunch plates. Instead of serving apple wedges and corn chips in bowls, the way I normally did for guests, I arranged them next to the pastrami sandwiches, the way I did when Bill was alive. I wasn't sure why.

While we ate on the front porch we made small talk, mostly about my drive to North Carolina the next morning to visit Michelle and her family. Jim leaned slightly forward and focused sharply on my face as he listened. Maybe he had a hearing

Chapter 18

problem? When we were done eating, I realized I hadn't planned for dessert. I felt terrible. Who invites someone over for a meal and doesn't serve dessert? I could only find three cinnamon cookies in the cupboard. They were long and narrow, so I broke each one in half and arranged them artfully on a small saucer.

I poked my head out the door. "Why don't we go to the side porch?"

Jim followed. We sat by the grill in deck chairs angled toward each other.

"It's beautiful here," Jim said. "I could stare at the woods for hours, probably from all the time I spend in tree stands. Or fishing."

I didn't say anything. I knew he had no clue he was looking at the spot where Bill died. In the two years and six months since the accident, I had sat in these chairs countless times, envisioning the police cars in the driveway, the priest offering the blessing, the assistant funeral director standing in a respectful stance at a respectful distance. I hadn't removed my hands from Bill's chest even after the crowd moved back. When I eventually turned away and headed up the stairs to the side porch, my niece, the nuns, and Father Mull followed. I'd watched the gurney slide into the hearse and stood motionless even after the taillights disappeared beyond the trees.

I'd rather not talk about the woods.

Squirrels scurried to collect beechnuts, and I steered the conversation toward innocuous things like the weather and our jobs. We talked easily as we nibbled on cookie fragments.

Until Jim pointed to the woods. "It's nice you have a bench out there."

I caught my breath and glanced over at the bench near the tree Bill was chopping when he died. If I'd come home earlier the day of the accident, when it was still light out, I would've seen him on the ground from the porch. I'd assembled the bench myself, shifting its weight against the dirt until the seat was level, and had tied bandanas—my yellow one, Bill's green one—to each side of the backrest. During Sister Dorothy's last visit, she said she wanted to see the bench up close. I was unsure about bringing her into the woods. She was unsteady on her feet on smooth ground. But hooking her arm to mine, she'd insisted. "I can feel Bill's love for you," she said when she sat down. "I know this will bring you peace." It felt like sacred ground there. On nice days I interrupted yardwork to visit. Sometimes I stopped by after dinner with a cup of coffee or tea. I had come to understand why people create roadside memorials, people like me who just want to be close to where their loved ones, without warning, took their last breath. Sometimes I could feel his arm around my waist, as if he were right there with me.

I sigh as quietly as I can.

"You probably heard what happened to my husband."

"I know something happened, but I don't know details."

My gaze wandered from the woods to the driveway and back to the woods as I spilled the story in a tone that felt safe—my voice measured, almost rote. When I got to the part about the blessing, I looked over at Jim. His eyes were watering.

I was overwhelming him.

I sighed again and softened my voice. "I know it's hard to hear."

"It is."

To keep from breaking down I changed the subject to Kilimanjaro, which we stayed on until Jim consulted his watch.

"I've been here three hours!" he exclaimed.

My eyes widened in shock. "I had no idea it was that late."

Where had the time gone?

"I'm going to scrub the rest of my plans and head home," he said, "My errands can wait."

I hoped he wouldn't regret the way things had panned out.

We took in our dishes and then, ready to leave, Jim walked toward the door. I felt awkward. I'd given this guy a hug at the end

Chapter 18

of every hike when everyone was hugging everybody. What was appropriate now?

I procrastinated. "Let me walk you out."

We talked by the car for a few minutes only to find ourselves in the exact same scenario. Jim didn't move. His hands were glued to his side.

"Well," I said, reaching my arms casually toward him. "Nice to see you."

He gave me a hug, a quick one, and got into his car.

I went back inside to finish packing for my trip to North Carolina. The task took only a few minutes because I'd started packing the week before, so I turned to tidying up. Coming home to a clean house was a special kind of gratification. When I was nearly done straightening the last of the catalogs, the phone rang. I heard Jim's voice and my stomach fluttered. Again, I wasn't sure why. He sounded serious. He said he'd thought a lot about the afternoon on his way home and had choked up thinking about what I'd been through.

"Thank you for opening up," he said. "It must've been hard to say all those things."

I was glad he noticed.

I replayed my call with Jim on my drive through Western New York, central Pennsylvania, Maryland, Virginia, and, at last, the outskirts of Raleigh, North Carolina. I wondered whether I'd hear from him while I was away. I was hoping I'd hear from him. Michelle was looking out for me when I arrived so I couldn't check my email as soon as I pulled into her driveway, as had been my plan over the past 600 miles. As hard as it was, I waited all afternoon, then all evening—until Michelle and her family were finally in bed—before scrolling through my email so quickly you'd think I was expecting to hear from my oncologist. Jim had, in fact, written earlier in the day, to thank me again. I wrote back and we continued emailing, though clandestinely on my end, throughout my visit. I didn't want Michelle asking questions because I wouldn't know what to say. And the fact that I wouldn't know what to say meant she'd have every right to ask questions. I didn't know what to think about the feelings that were cropping up. I knew Bill was aware they existed, but at no point did I feel an ounce of betrayal in my bones.

At one point in our exchanges, I invited Jim to dinner.

"Do you want to cook on the grill?" I wrote.

He answered, "That's one art I've chosen not to learn all that well. But I could probably figure it out."

I spent the car ride home smiling at the thought of Jim back at my house. But the next week, about 15 minutes before he really would be at my house, I was nothing but nerves. I dashed around downstairs, triple-checking that there was no sign of clutter and wondering whether I should've spent more time on my hair. Good thing I'd just had it colored.

After setting steaks and tongs on a platter beside the grill, I gave myself a third—maybe fourth—once-over in the bedroom mirror. I felt respectably casual in capris, a knit top, and sandals. Bill had always stood at the mirror longer than I would, running his hands through his thick black hair. "Don't I look nice?" he'd ask until he got a reaction. I never dawdled in front of my reflection, but that was precisely what I was doing. I glanced at the smudges on the mirror, then stared straight into my own eyes.

I hadn't done this in 30 years.

When Michelle called earlier, I told her only that a hiker friend was coming over for dinner. There was no mention of a date.

Was it okay that this was a date?

The alarm sounded. Jim had pulled into the driveway.

I greeted him at the side porch.

"I thought I'd bring you something for your deck," he said,

Chapter 18

hauling a monstrous chestnut-colored mum from the back seat of his car.

"It's beautiful. Thank you." I made a semi-circle with my arms to grab the pot and set the plant next to my other mums. They were dwarfed by the gift.

"Everything's ready to go," I said, pointing to the steaks and tongs next to the grill. "I'll be right back with drinks. What would you like?"

"A beer would be great if you have one."

Inside, I cracked open a beer for Jim and poured myself a glass of Jameson Irish whiskey. By the time I returned to the porch with the drinks and some snacks, Jim had lit the grill and was inspecting the steaks.

"Time to get to work," he said.

At 6 feet tall, Bill had towered over the grill. Jim was 5'3", about an inch shorter than I was. The height difference between them made my stomach drop. I took a hard sip of whiskey.

"This is fancy," Jim said, tapping the tongs against the grill pan full of onions, peppers, and garlic. "I'm used to tinfoil."

He turned around. I don't know what I was expecting, but not seeing Bill's round face and high forehead took me by surprise.

Bill, you're not here.

Again, I lifted the glass to my lips.

Jim is a good guy, right?

Another sip of whiskey.

Is it okay to remember what used to be?

I swallowed.

Jim turned toward me. "So, tell me more about your trip."

I could tell from his locked gaze that his interest was genuine, which put me at ease. I reached for a cheese-topped cracker and took my time rehashing the past few days swimming and playing games in the back yard with Katie.

When the steaks were almost done, I went to the refrigerator for the German potato salad I'd made often over the past two decades but not since Bill died. Bill's grandmother had given me the recipe—a simple pairing of potatoes, salt, pepper, oil, and vinegar. Bill would sit at the kitchen counter with a fork and taste my attempts to get it just right. Inevitably I'd need more of one ingredient or another. This afternoon I'd had to guess.

Jim did a good job with the steaks, and the next four hours vanished without me even once checking the time. After dinner we split an enormous slice of carrot cake—I was prepared for dessert this time—before facing another potentially awkward departure. I'd already decided to make the first move faster this time. I gave Jim a short hug in the living room as we traded goodbyes.

"This feels really good," Jim said. "I'd like to do it again."

I didn't know exactly what felt good to him. Our night together? The hug? Both? But it was enough information to unleash a swarm of butterflies in my belly.

"Me too."

I was feeling more comfortable with this man by the minute.

Chapter 19

I emerge from my tent beneath a clear blue sky, the sun peeking over the snow-dotted mountain peak.

Yesterday's brown crewneck has been swapped for a red turtleneck and heavier pants have replaced thinner ones. By repeating the same morning routine as planned, I was able to dress quickly for the day's four-hour hike—so quickly that on my way to the food tent I pat my pockets to confirm I haven't forgotten my toilet paper baggies.

I'm surprisingly hungry after last night's spread of chapati with shredded chicken and melted cheese, rice, carrot-ginger soup, and mixed vegetables.

I make short work of the toast and eggs, pausing mid-meal only to take my vitamins and medicine with Milo-spiked coffee instead of on an empty stomach to help avoid another race to the woods. I think the problem yesterday was that I'd downed all those pills before breakfast. At least I hope that was the problem yesterday.

Once fueled, I find my refilled water bottle and hydration pack on a tarp outside the food tent. The pick-up is timed perfectly, and probably on purpose, for Yusuf's pronouncement.

"Mohammed is ready!"

The lead guide stands perfectly still, quiet, solid—a metronome before it does its work.

Already lathered up with sunscreen, I slip on sunglasses and join Sue at the end of the line, where she is collecting data on her oxygen levels and other vital signs to use when teaching residents at the medical center where she works. She and Kevin got to talking yesterday and discovered they'd both graduated from the same medical school nearly a decade apart.

The other Mohammed, the sweeper at the back of the pack, doesn't say much on the trail—partly because he's shy, partly because his English is spotty at best. That doesn't stop the most inquisitive climbers from asking him loads of personal questions, for which I'm thankful because I want to soak up as much knowledge as I can about those charged with keeping us alive. From what we can gather, this Mohammed hopes his work as a mountain guide will help him afford an irrigation system for his farm near the Indian Ocean. He waters crops by hand now. Impressive. The only thing I water by hand are my houseplants, and that's hard enough to remember to do.

It occurs to me that we still haven't come across any elephants. The altitude may be too high for them at this point, although according to the Chagga people, when Kilimanjaro elephants sense their time has come, they make their way to the edge of a mysterious crater hidden by snowdrifts farther up the mountain. The elephants jump to their death, the legend goes, to foil poachers. Tons and tons of elephant remains are said to be nearly unreachable. Those who do stumble upon this final resting place are reportedly cursed, either with sudden blindness or eternity inside the crater. That's what I love about legends—whether or not they're plausible, they give me something to contemplate.

Before noon we move into the moorland. It's mostly a gentle walk. The trail is lined with tiny rocks that look like haphazardly spread gravel and make a crunching sound when disturbed. We pass mossy streams, small alpine flowers, and dramatic red hot peppers with flowers so bright they're blazing like hot metal straight out of the forge. Perennial succulents known as Senecio Kilimanjaro have thick, silvery, needle-like leaves that would look stunning in a porch container garden.

Then the scenery turns psychedelic. A peculiar collection of giant groundsel plants resemble overgrown pineapples-on-a-stick, some nearly 30 feet tall.

"I feel like I'm in a Dr. Seuss book," Phil says, his eyes wide with childlike wonder. "This is the kind of stuff he must've seen in his head."

I'm not a fan. The odd plants look out of place and make me feel even farther away from home. They remind me of how uneasy I felt in Romania last year because the trees in the forests grew differently there. They thrived despite being crammed so tightly you'd get lost five feet inside the darkness. How can you trust a place that doesn't make sense? Without an answer, I lean on what I know to be true—that I am not lost and am among friends who will make sure I stay that way.

We stop for a snack break and more sunscreen. The rainforest had protected us from the merciless African sun but here, fully overhead, it emphatically demands attention. Only after confirming I've brought enough peanut-butter-and-cheese crackers do I notice the charred branches and shrubs. Yusuf calls us together and points to the landscape.

"Forest fire," he says. The blaze was started by a thoughtlessly discarded cigarette. Flames swept across the mountain's upper slopes during a dry spell and caused considerable damage. Twenty-two men, all squatters and identified as culprits by secret ballot, were arrested for their part in the destruction.

Yusuf doesn't like that this is the type of story that too often makes worldwide news.

"CNN forgets about the peaceful Tanzania, but look here," he says, peering at new plants sprouting between the scorched remains. Ironically, they are known as everlasting flowers.

Yellowish-brown and lemon-scented, their stiff structure allows them to bloom year-round, even through frosty nights and with little water.

Yusuf talks often about the love he has for his country and this mountain. The swift pace of American life holds no appeal for him, that much was clear from stories of his first visit to the United States. "Yes, you have lots to eat," he'd told Rick during that stay, "but no time to eat it." Rick was newly divorced and broke at the time he'd cobbled together enough money to buy Yusuf's plane ticket. It was mid-November in Upstate New York, where daytime temperatures hovered around 40 degrees—not an easy adjustment for an African. But that was the only time Rick had a break from his travels and Yusuf had less work on the mountain since Kilimanjaro was colder and windier than average that time of year. Rick was living in a rustic two-room cabin five miles down a dirt road, then another 300 yards down a hill and behind a barn. The hill had to be traversed on foot and the cabin wasn't in the best shape. Wind howled through cracks in the windowpanes. Yusuf slept in the loft, above the woodstove, where it was warmest. When it was too cold to walk to the outhouse, the men used a bucket and plastic lid just like on the mountain. During the day, in exchange for donations, Yusuf gave presentations to business groups and adventure clubs about life as a Tanzanian mountain guide. At night the men shoveled snow off the pond by the barn to play hockey, cooked turkeys on a camping stove, and hauled in supplies by sled. When he missed home, Yusuf got on his hands and knees to wash the wood floor with an old towel the same way he did in Africa. Rick adopted the ritual after Yusuf left, washing the floor on all fours every two weeks to remind himself to be humble. Yusuf wound up with $2,000 in donations over the six weeks he stayed with Rick—roughly a year's salary back home. He used the money to fix up his house and buy a plot of land next door to build the house his family lives in now.

Since we've stopped walking, the mountain air feels colder. I

Chapter 19

shove the plastic wrap from the crackers into my pocket and reach for my camera.

"Yusuf, can I take your picture? You too, Mohammed."

The men oblige. Yusuf flashes his easy smile. Lead guide Mohammed again stands with his arms crossed, expressionless.

"Asante sana," I say.

"No worries," Yusuf replies. "Onward!"

I pull my buff up from my neck and over my nose to ward off the trail dust, now swirling even more relentlessly with each step. Not that we need something else to make it harder to breathe. The increasing elevation requires us to inhale more often just to get the same amount of oxygen we had at lower altitudes. On a physiological level, our bodies are creating more and more red blood cells to shuttle oxygen through the bloodstream, pushing air into parts of our lungs we don't normally use. I can't think about that for too long or my breath becomes even more labored. It doesn't help that the Kibo summit, rising more than a mile high in front of us, looks more imminent and threatening than ever.

It's baffling how the mountain can be so mercurial. One moment the summit commands the landscape, mammoth and unyielding, only to become an ephemeral mirage the next. Visible from a hundred miles away, invisible even as you're on it when the clouds roll in. Now I know why Hemingway once wrote that in Africa something is true at dawn but a lie by noon.

The weather is moody. Warm, then chilly, then warm. Jacket off, jacket on, jacket off.

Even flat portions of the trail leave me winded. When I stop walking to chug some water, I must take a deep breath afterward to recover from the break from breathing I had to take in order to swallow.

"Pole-ay, pole-ay!" Rick's voice reaches my ears from far ahead, the words exaggerated.

Slowly, slowly.

What would I do without Rick here? These types of trips—on

unpredictable mountains and susceptible to unpredictable circumstances—are in his constitution. Now married again, he's away on one odyssey or another as many as 22 weeks a year. It's a schedule he says suits his wife just fine. She prefers structure and order, while he's apt to dump his jacket on the floor on his way to the computer to nail down a bush plane pick-up. That doesn't mean the plane will show up on time, of course, but Rick doesn't come undone. "Do you worry," he has said, "or do you pick blueberries and savor the flavor of the only food you have?" I know two things. There is no way on God's green earth I could savor anything in that situation, and I would want to be with someone who could.

As we climb higher, the black, pockmarked rocks on the trail are getting larger and there's more snow on the mountain. Another burst of sun, another rest. A couple men flex muscles as they pose for pictures. I join some of the women for a communal bathroom break behind the biggest boulder we can find. I wish the terrain cared more about modesty.

No sooner are we walking again than the mountain becomes shrouded in thick clouds strewn like stretched-out cotton balls. The shrubs look ashen, and I can barely detect the yellow flowers on spindly, trailside bushes. By the time we descend a deep ravine and reach the rusted ranger hut at the edge of Shira 2 Camp where we're sleeping tonight, the temperature is noticeably cooler, though it's only early afternoon. I wrap my buff around my head for added insulation just as hail begins to fall. My sweat-covered body tenses against the unexpected frozen pellets. Someone shouts that we've reached 12,600 feet in just under four hours. I pay more attention to the time than the altitude. Yusuf had said we would be walking two or three hours today but I hadn't once checked my watch, so maybe my body is equipped for this trip after all. Or maybe time on the mountain is as fluid as the weather.

Our tents are pitched in moorland meadows by a stream. I'm past ready for a meal but lunch isn't ready, so while waiting I

Chapter 19

upgrade to fleece-lined hiking pants. Sue rifles through her bag in a frantic search the entire time it takes me to change. It pains my organizational sensitivities to watch her clothes fly around the tent.

"What are you searching for?"

"Socks."

I hand Sue the pair of socks that had landed on my sleeping bag and fish out Bill's black down coat from my own duffel. I'd decided to bring his coat the morning I started sorting through his things. That chore had been long overdue but I thought that maybe, by holding off for 18 months, it might be a less arduous one. I was still touching and smelling his clothes in our walk-through closet as I breezed into the bathroom each morning and shuffled to bed each night. Some days I could imagine us still living together and some days it seemed he had been gone for decades. The furthest I had pushed myself to that point had been to take over his drawers in our dresser. They were higher and had more room than my drawers at the bottom. Months later I went through his wardrobe. In the end, I dropped off several bulging extra-large trash bags to a charity resale shop and gifted his favorite shirts to one of Bill's closest friends and to my niece's husband. I kept two coats, a black one and a brown one, and two shirts—a pastel pink Oxford and a neon orange hiking shirt. The pink one looked good with Bill's black hair and made me think about how he'd bulk up his muscles in front of the mirror, playfully gloating about how manly he looked. As for the hiking shirt, he proudly wore it nonstop on our 10-day rafting trip along Alaska's Sagavanirkt River. He got so much attention early on for wearing the same shirt every day that I knew it wasn't coming off.

We hear a call from outside. "Lunch is almost ready!"

I jot a quick note to Jim in my journal.

I'm doing well. I miss you and look forward to us seeing each other tomorrow when our routes converge. Love, Bonnie

I tear out the page and stick it in one of Bill's coat pockets.

I drape the coat over one arm and push myself up.

"See you soon," I say to Sue.

"See you soon," she says. "Thanks for the socks."

I put on the coat the moment I'm outside where there is more room to stretch. I always have to be careful when I stretch. If I bend over too long, a searing pain wrenches my gut, a lingering side effect of the radiation.

My body moves around freely in Bill's coat. It's much too big on me but that's sort of the point. I like the slack of it, the way it makes me think of his long body and broad shoulders.

I look around for Rick or Matt, the guy from the American Cancer Society. They're planning a quick visit to the Machame group campsite about a half hour's walk to the south.

Rick is near the cook's tent. I hold out my note. "Can you give this to Jim?"

Rick puts the note in his coat pocket. "Aw, just like junior high."

I smile wryly. "I'm going to eat now."

On one of our Friday training hikes, Sue had said, "Hey, Jim stayed at your house after everyone left last week. What was that all about?" Grateful that Jim was out of earshot—though by this point I knew he needed hearing aids—I answered, "He invited me out for coffee. A couple days ago he came over for dinner. We're getting to know each other." Sue stared ahead and walked briskly. "You must've had a good marriage to feel comfortable enough to start another relationship," she said. Relationship? I bristled at the word. Jim and I may have had coffee and dinner together in a short amount of time, but we most certainly were not in a relationship. Just hearing the word made me want to apologize to Bill.

Not long after, things changed. After another large-group training hike, Jim asked if I wanted to check out a new cafe down the road. My piano teacher had canceled our lesson so I had the time. Over coffee and pastries, Jim told me about his recent retirement after 32 years at Kodak and about his stint in the Marines. He'd requested to go to Vietnam out of anger after his older brother lost a leg there. It was as if we'd shifted into new territory when he told me that last part. We started talking on the phone every day and emailed almost as much. I loved the way Jim approached things—slowly. He didn't come right out and ask, "Do you want to go for a hike?" Instead he would describe a trail, including tiny streams and other geographic details, then ask what I thought about joining him. And he was always a perfect gentleman. Just before our first kiss he'd shifted his weight repeatedly from one foot to the other. I could feel the tension mount. His eyes were watery. Wanting to put him out of his misery I reached for his hand, gave it a squeeze, and said, "I'd like to keep seeing you." With shaky words, he asked for permission to kiss me. I leaned in. The kiss was short but memorable, awakening in me a vaguely familiar sense of happiness. I had been relieved to be intimate again with someone, even if that intimacy was innocent and fleeting. He'd called me after that kiss, once he got home, to thank me for taking his hand.

I'm hoping Jim had a good day on the mountain.

Sadie, her hair in long braids, is in one corner of the food tent recording an audio post on Rick's satellite phone for the Journeys of Inspiration website. She's talking about a close friend who had a bone marrow transplant last week. "If she can stay strong through that," she says, staring at the ground, "we can stay strong through anything we face up here."

Sadie's comment makes my eyes tear up and I feel a sudden urge to look at my banner. It's still at the bottom of my daypack. Lunch can wait. Walking back to the tent, I make a mental note to put on more layers. The wind has changed from gnawing to biting.

Sue is gone—she's probably in the toilet tent since I didn't pass her—and it's just as well. I feel like the banner needs my full attention. I sweep my eyes over messages written on my behalf by people who made donations to the American Cancer Society in support of this climb. In black ink there are celebratory words from a group of breast cancer survivors: "You go girl!" and "I'm still alive!" There are tributes to a ninth-grade English teacher and a four-year-old. A couple's chant: "Cancer can be beaten! Cancer must be beaten! Cancer will be beaten!" And a heart. The woman who drew it is a Serenity House volunteer whose teenage nephew died of cancer. "I never thought he would climb Kilimanjaro, and now he's going to do it," she had said before writing his name next to the heart.

In writing slanted to the right is my note to Jim:

To our journey.

With love,
Bonnie

Above it, in writing slanted to the left, is my message to Bill:

I will always know
and feel your love.
It is your strength
that will carry me.

My love to you,
Bonnie

I don't know what I would do if I didn't believe Bill was in this place with me. At this very moment.

The cook, Raziki, sticks his head into the tent during dinner. Like Yusuf, he is from the Pare tribe. They've worked together for five years. We've noticed the two of them slip into their

Chapter 19

mother tongue when they don't want Rick to know what they're saying.

"How is everything?" Raziki asks.

Ravenous after a too-light lunch of salad, french fries, and banana fritters, we respond with nods and pleasurable moans. Tonight he has made pasta with stewed meat, soup, and papayas. Satisfied, Raziki smiles and heads back to the kitchen tent, its torn top secured with twine. I'm amazed he can whip up such carefully composed meals in there.

"How does he do it?" I mutter to no one in particular. I don't know how the natives do anything in this weather—now below freezing—without the benefit of thermal base layers and insulated outerwear.

Rick must've heard me. He puts down his fork. "The ground in the kitchen is littered with broken-down cardboard boxes and tiny slivers of carrot, potato, and onion peels."

The table grows quiet. Rick goes on to explain that Raziki shares the space with an assistant cook and two helpers, one of which is a server also named Mohammed. A few porters usually hang around to drink tea and gossip. Raziki stations himself in a corner in front of two rusty propane stoves. While cooking for us, he makes a separate pot of ugali for himself and the other Africans using a

hand-carved wooden spoon with a severed handle. There's no room in the budget for them to eat anything else. The knives, in better shape than the spoon, are sharpened by a guy who occasionally stops by the Springlands Hotel with his bicycle and a triangular metal stand.

Rick pauses, grins, and leans in as if he's about to deliver a punchline. "The guy on the bicycle," he says, "runs a rubber belt from a small grinding stone to a small extension on the hub of the back wheel. Sitting backward on his seat, he sharpens the knives as he pedals."

It all sounds straight out of a novel, though it does make me think of Romania. In a country where half the land is deemed agricultural, I saw not one tractor or other piece of automated equipment the entire eight days we were there. I did see women and children heaping hay together in flawless stacks—a sight that made me nostalgic. In the United States we tend to reap the benefits of time-saving technology by spending even more time with technology.

My mind loops details from Romania and Raziki's tent until I take my last bite. I slide my chair back to stand just as Matt, seated farther down the table, calls my name.

"Here's something from Jim," he says with a wink, pulling a folded index card from his coat pocket.

I open the note straightaway.

Bonnie,
I also love you and miss you. Got misty eyes when I got your note. Doing great. No Diamox yet. Heavy rain yesterday. Late to camp — 6:30 p.m. Frost &
ICE on tents this morning. Hail this afternoon for short while. Awesome team.

Love, Jim

I'm barely finished reading when the banter starts.

"What does the lovebird have to say?"

"How sappy did he get?"

"You guys are so cute!"

I lean back in my chair and let the chatter recede into unintelligible white noise. Jim is doing well. Still, the mother in me can't let one thing go. How come he hasn't started taking his Diamox?

I don't have time to ponder the question. The tent flaps open to a chorus of clapping porters backlit by the moon. In sweatpants and layered jerseys, unaffected by the frosty

Chapter 19

temperature, the men cavort and whirl against a sky of shadows as they sing:

Jambo
Jambo Bwana
Habari gani
Mzuri Sana
Wageni
Mwakaribishwa
Kilimanjaro
Hakuna Matata

Greetings
Hello Mister
How are you
Very fine
Foreigners
You are welcome
Kilimanjaro
No worries

We join them in the clapping from our seats. My smile couldn't be bigger.

When the serenade is over, we cheer and bombard the men with questions.

"Can you sing to us every night after dinner?"

"What about in the morning to help us out of our tents?"

The porters smile without answering, the way people do when they want to be polite but not commit to anything. Some of them wave and the tent flaps close—but only for a moment before Yusuf joins us.

He asks for our attention. "Everything good so far?"

We cheer.

"You feel this is not a punishment? Just a holiday?"

We cheer again.

"It is my pleasure to hear that," he says. "Now we have to prepare for our hike tomorrow."

It will be a long day—seven or eight hours to the campsite at Barranco Hut. At a mid-afternoon lunch stop we'll meet up with the Machame group and have the option to continue climbing to the base of Lava Tower, a 300-foot-tall volcanic rock formation thousands of years old. Going to Lava Tower, at just over 15,000 feet, will help our bodies acclimate before returning to Barranco Camp at a much lower altitude. Or we can proceed directly to camp.

Without a doubt I want to go to Lava Tower. I want my body to be as primed as possible to handle the higher altitudes and lower oxygen levels to come. I'm confident Jim will feel the same way.

"The wind will be stronger so balaclavas and gloves go in daypacks," Yusuf continues. "Tightened boots will prevent blisters. Trekking poles will relieve pressure on knees."

I already have problems with my knees and have been postponing a doctor's visit and likely diagnosis of osteoarthritis, an affliction that affected much of my maternal side of the family and caused my mother to walk like a duck. I'll be sure to have my poles at the ready.

"Any questions?"

No one pipes up.

"Well then, asante sana and lala salama." Yusuf backs out of the tent and into a gentle rain.

"Lala salama," I say, the syllables tumbling out in a slur. I guess after all the walking, and feeling relieved that Jim is doing well, my body is shutting down for the night.

I think I'll sleep in Bill's coat, wrapped in what he used to touch, the material a tangible token of his support.

Chapter 20

One night soon after Bill died, I saw a long flash of light while driving home on a dark country road. The flash—literally coming from somewhere out of left field—illuminated a man walking alone. He was hunched over, weighed down by a backpack that seemed too small for his frame. Whatever journey he was on looked difficult. The light disappeared when I passed him, leaving only the mysterious night in my rearview mirror. But I could still picture the man vividly. He'd looked so much like Bill—the same shape, the same bend in his back as he hiked. Maybe it really had been Bill, sending another sign. Like the tears on my bedroom mirror. Or when I smelled roses when they weren't around, a reminder of the surprise bouquets he used to bring home.

The night had been atrocious. I'd gone to an American Cancer Society Relay for Life fundraising walk, even though I wasn't in the mood, because my niece Annie wanted me there. She'd made sure I was given a survivor's T-shirt to wear and that one of the luminaries lighting the track we walked around had my name on it. All well-intentioned and sweet, but the whoops and applause from observers felt incongruous with my waves of sadness, steady and grating as a slow drip.

I was grieving. The last thing I wanted was a cheering section.

Once home I parked the car and headed straight upstairs to get ready for bed. Unclasping the pewter cross necklace I bought Bill early in our marriage, I was hit with an image so clear it made me dash downstairs, the necklace still in my hand. I flipped through photo albums until I found the picture I was after—one of Bill leaning forward with his back to the camera, his rounded shoulders strapped to a backpack. I stared at the picture a long time, convinced that in some way the stooped man on the side of the road was indeed a sign.

I looked up at the ceiling.

Bill, you would've known what an awful night this was. You're still here for me.

Chapter 21

It's too early to be this cold. I went to sleep with a hat, gloves, extra layers of clothing, and Bill's coat only to shake through the night.

I can think of nothing but a litany of complaints. I desperately need a shower. I miss Bloomfield. I miss Bill. He would have taken good care of me here, and I'm tired of doing everything myself.

Even knowing that I'll be seeing Jim today, I have no desire to start my morning routine. And I won't be getting any nudging from Sue. She's not here, so I assume she's already at breakfast.

Sluggish in my sleeping bag, I place my palm against the medallion around my neck. The medallion is like a security blanket in moments like this, its tribal face a symbol of another man who has my back—Rick's younger brother, Steve. The two of them are a lot alike. Short, fit, funny. Steve helped lead the trip to Romania. On a sunset hike there he showed me the medallion he wore, the one he used as a talisman on his second climb up Kilimanjaro two years before. "I never take this off," he said. I was intrigued by the idea of a talisman. I'd always used prayer when wanting protection and good luck. He assured me I wouldn't have any problems with my climb as long as I listened to the guides, walked slowly, and drank lots of water. Then he said, "It will change you." When I got home from Romania and unpacked my suitcase, Steve's medallion was at the bottom. I found out later he'd snuck it in there during our last breakfast, after finding my bag stacked with the others near the hotel entrance. He'd wrapped it in a note that said, in part, that when I hear "Jambo!" I should remember he wishes me well and is thinking of me on the mountain. The medallion and "the power it holds," he wrote, "are now yours, forever!"

I frequently go back to that moment—to that vacation in general, like I did last night at dinner—for inspiration. It had been a big deal for me to go overseas by myself. I was still feeling alone in a crowd, as if I were outside a bubble I couldn't penetrate. I even paid extra for a single room. I wasn't ready to wear pajamas and brush my teeth around a stranger. My first night in Romania, at a long table in the back of a restaurant, I was surrounded mostly by couples and feeling out of place. Then on the menu I spotted chicken paprikash, a Hungarian staple and one of the dishes Bill's grandmother had taught me to cook. Instantly I felt better, as if Bill had placed a light, invisible blanket on my lap. I ordered the dish that night and any other night I found it on a restaurant menu. We spent our days walking through immaculate villages and rugged farmland. At a half-built monastery with turrets and crosses cut into concrete pillars, we lit tall, thin candles stuck in dirt-filled pie plates. We set the plates at the feet of a grey-haired woman, signaling our request to participate in a prayer service. The woman closed her eyes and we closed ours and at the sound of her velvety voice, the whole world became a little easier to manage. When I opened my eyes, even though I didn't fully grasp it at the time, I'd begun to feel a change already.

"Knock, knock." I recognize Linda Number One's voice outside my tent.

"Morning." I sit up. "Come in."

Linda Number One unzips the tent just enough to accommodate her head. She looks at my neat side and Sue's not-so-neat side, and laughs. "Glad to see you're making it work. Ready for breakfast?"

I hold up a finger. "I'll be right there. Just need to get my things together."

"Take your time. I'll save you a seat."

I stuff the day's supplies in my pack and wipe a wet cloth over my face to little reward. I guess I can't expect much else after four days on the mountain.

In the food tent, I feel even more sticky and slimy with Kim looking stylish in her hoop earrings. An unusually passionate debate is brewing over the quality of the runny, russet-colored porridge. I sort of like the consistency but keep that to myself. The gruel had comforted my stomach after retching the other morning and comforts me still. I'm feeling less crabby by the spoonful. I'd even go so far as to call the porridge a daily epicurean delight—a warm, nutty, soothing balm reminding my system each morning that all is well. I have a thing for repetition. Bill used to tease me about always wanting to go to the same restaurant for dinner when it was my turn to choose. What can I say? I like knowing what to expect.

Accustomed to the morning regimen by now, we are all done with breakfast and on the trail more quickly today, buoyed by a blue sky with puffy clouds and eager for our upcoming reunion with the Machame group.

The terrain is changing again. We pass giant lobelia, an otherworldly endemic plant with concave spiky leaves artfully arranged to trap rainwater. And soon the open moorlands fade away, replaced by sage grass, hearty helichrysum flowers, moss, and thistles that announce the arid alpine desert region. Just thinking about the word "desert" makes me reach for my water bottle—not that I've ever been in a desert this chilly.

"Porter on the left!" a high-pitched voice blares from behind.

I step to the right. The first porter who passes is young and well built. He keeps his right hand in his pocket. With his left hand he steadies a stack of plastic chairs, wrapped in a bright orange tarp, on his back. The porter behind him balances a full sack on his head. It occurs to me that I haven't seen the sick teenage boy since our first day.

I'm not feeling so great anymore myself. Just 45 minutes on the trail—nothing but uphill today from the get-go—fog and wind have replaced the blue sky, and I'm shivering despite being in both my fleece jacket and Bill's coat. The shudders take me back to the Adirondacks, to a solo trip I took last year to prove to myself that I could hike alone in foreign territory. At the end of one trail east of Tupper Lake—an easy, scenic four-mile walk that crossed a Norway spruce plantation—I rested on a flat rock by a pond, letting my hums waft over the water. Wanting to write to Bill, I rummaged through my backpack for my journal and pen.

I tried to be positive. *The sweet side is how intensely I love you.*

I tried to be assuring. *My faith makes me believe that our love in heaven will be beyond my imagination. God would not give us each other on this earth and then take it all away…*

I searched for meaning. *It feels a little chilly with the breeze hitting my face. I always remember you telling me how when you shiver, it makes you feel alive. Are you trying to tell me to feel alive?*

I pull on gloves and wrap my buff around my head in a way that makes it resemble the balaclava in my pack. The actual balaclava would be better, but I can't even think about stopping to fish it out. I need to keep moving, to keep sending oxygen to my cells and blood to my organs. I try to ignore the rumbles in my stomach. I should've eaten more at breakfast.

Cloaked in haze, my eyelids start to sag. Paul darts to the front of the line to film each of us as we pass. How is it humanly possible to move that fast right now? Standing to the side of the trail, he peppers us with questions, his voice exuberant. I feel a titch irritated, probably because I'm hungry and tired.

That I'm going to see Jim this afternoon keeps me going more than anything. I poke along the steep trail, now nothing but ashen

Chapter 21

sand, past tiers of black rocks dripping with thin strands of yellowish-orange moss. The moss looks like string confetti tossed to celebrate our arrival. Nothing is green anymore.

I steady myself against a large boulder to maneuver over several smaller ones in my way and notice a stretcher off the trail—a discomforting sight and blatant reminder of the trip's hazards. I miss my family. I don't usually miss them when I travel. This mountain is a different beast for so many reasons.

It helps to know that Yusuf misses his family too. He talks freely about his wife and biological son, as well as the son and two nieces he adopted. He says he makes sacrifices to be on the mountain during tourist season. One of them is being away from his wife's banana soup.

"And I do not pray five times a day when I am in the field," he admits. By field, I guess he means the mountain. "But always, if I am in any other place, I do."

I'm praying that I get more pep in my step soon.

"Yusuf, tell us another story," I plead.

He dives right in. When Yusuf was in his early 20s, his parents thought it was time for him to marry. As a dutiful son, he agreed to meet with three women his mother identified as potential mates, though he wasn't ready to wed and had no plans to propose. The first woman made it clear she was ready to become his wife, but Yusuf found her rather homely. He spent hours with her, nervously trying to figure out how to present himself as an unappealing suitor. When she asked about his job, he knew he had found a way out. In his village the poorest families sell tiny, dry fish. Yusuf knew that an auction to buy the fish was that weekend in another town, so he told her she'd better make up her mind about marrying him quickly because he had to prepare for the trip. The woman had an abrupt change of heart and said she wasn't ready to marry after all. "I have a lot to do," she told him. "I have to go to school." A triumphant Yusuf set down his cup of tea and left. After meeting the other two prospects, he broke the news to his mother that he was to remain a bachelor, at least for a while. "The first one was the best, but she was just looking for someone with money," he said, adding that he wasn't interested in that type of relationship. His mother couldn't blame him for that. His parents had given up on finding him a wife when he fell in love with Fatma. "She was the right choice," he says. "She is cute and works hard."

Hearing about Yusuf's relationship makes me think about mine. It feels like an unbelievably long time since Jim and I have seen each other. He has always been the more patient one. Come to think of it, so was Bill. On one of our three-day canoe trips in the Adirondacks, the portages between inlets were tough, some a mile long. I walked ahead along one of them. The plan was for me to shout back to Bill, who was carrying our canoe overhead, once I'd identified a place to camp. After no luck I retraced my steps and found Bill stuck in the mud up to his knees. He'd never shouted for me to turn back. He'd just waited.

I'm starting to feel cranky again. This desert doesn't have any heat and I'm annoyed that I can't quench my thirst no matter how much water I drink. I thank God when the Machame hikers appear on a distant ridge. Some of them stand on rocks like sentries. One is in fluorescent orange—the color of Jim's coat. My heartbeat picks up pace and my feet follow, kicking up dust more quickly now despite the small stones that have started to cover the powdery path.

Others reach the Machame hikers before I do. I can hear Elizabeth saying we looked like a long caterpillar when she first spotted our Lemosho line, there were so many of us on the trail. I wonder if she ever got her luggage. I reach out for Jim as soon as he is close enough to touch. The beard he'd started growing back home to prepare for summit night pricks my lips when we kiss.

"Hello, trail angel," he says.

I love when he calls me that. When I mentioned during one of our hiking dates that my maiden name is Angel, Jim asked if I knew about trail angels. I didn't. He told me the term officially refers to volunteers who provide long-distance hikers with anything from a beer to a bed, but that Jack had expanded the definition after Jim's divorce. On Jim's behalf, Jack would size up the women they passed on any number of mountains, then ask Jim whether he could envision her as a potential wife—his trail angel. "I always believed I'd find her," Jim had said on our date. I didn't know if he meant me, but I liked the implication.

Both clans start to razz us.

"He's so mellow now," the guys taunt.

The women follow suit. "Look, she's swooning!"

Jim's cheeks turn pink. I think the jeers are sophomoric and wonderful.

I notice the food tent. "C'mon," I say. "Let's eat."

"We ate earlier," Jim says. "You go ahead. I'll tag along."

Rick is already inside the tent. He gives those of us climbing to Lava Tower an update on weather conditions. "Be prepared to be wet and cold."

I'm already cold and don't want to get wet.

"Dress like you would for summit night," Yusuf adds.

I'm shivering again, more from the thought of what the afternoon holds than from the stinging chill in the air. If the idea of Lava Tower makes me feel this way, how am I going to handle summit night?

Chapter 22

Journal in my lap, I sat against a birch tree near Long Pond in the Adirondacks. I wrote to Bill about being back at our favorite wilderness campsite where we used to go on a whim for the weekend.

Bill, our special place looks beautiful today.

I'd gone back there alone, for the first time, the year before. The site had been filthy, littered with strips of torn toilet paper. With my hands around a lukewarm cup of gas station coffee, I'd stood there and cried. It had felt good to cry that long and that hard without anyone around to hear.

I hadn't come back for closure or to cling to the past. Instead, starting an unprecedented solo hiking trip first in the Adirondacks, then in Maine, I wanted to reconnect with the places that brought me joy. Little by little, that emotion had become increasingly recognizable since my phone call with Rick about Kilimanjaro. The trip was six months away.

This is almost the hardest moment I've had without you, I wrote.

There, at the campsite, I could picture us so clearly—heating water over the two-burner camping stove, washing dishes, and burrowing under blankets in the truck bed under the stars, safeguarded from the evening chill. I could almost feel the tin cup of tea in my hand. Bill's cup would've been on the table he'd fashioned from a camp stool and square chunk of metal from the basement. He was known for his frugality—one of the reasons his restaurant of choice was Cheap Charlie's. The man never threw anything away. Flat metal pieces from old computer printers became dustpans for the litter box, and all he had to do to fix a plumbing problem was sift through his extensive collection of scraps. At the library two days before he died, I recognized the long, T-shaped piece of plastic piping attached to the key to the bathroom. "This used to be in my garage, didn't it?" I'd asked. The librarian confirmed the donation had come from Bill.

It's still so hard for me to think about our memories. I don't know why I'm afraid to remember. I just am... Thank you for holding me up.

After committing to Kilimanjaro I was deliberate in my return to the trail, starting with clearing a new walking path in the woods next to my house. In an old shirt and jeans, I began at the north end of the property trimming budding bushes and marking sensible intervals with orange surveyor's tape. Next I moved west. When I came to a swampy area I did my best with the rocks within reach to create a path over the squishiest parts. Deeper in I turned south, looking back to make sure I could see the last knot of tape through the trees. Then east, back through the mush and prickly underbrush and into the side yard. I was at ease in the woods again and felt ready to hit the trails in nearby Boughton Park. It would be a homecoming of sorts. On the trail I knew the season by sound alone—the rustling wind in spring, the harmonic warbling of the wood thrush in summer, the leaves hitting the forest floor in autumn, the crunch of snow in winter. The consistency was comforting. When thinking about the landscape, how what was there had been there for ages and would be there for ages, it was easier to characterize everything else—doubts, insecurities, sadness—as irrelevant. In the woods I could unburden my mind until only the towering trunks of the trees, then the branches on the trees, then the leaves on the branches, then the veins on the leaves came into focus, and there was nothing but beauty in the world. But when I got to the park, the familiar turned foreign. The trees seemed much taller than before, and I could no longer anticipate the path's next bend. I longed to hear Bill's huge hiking boots clomping behind me. Just shy of a mile in, kids swung from a rope into a pond. They were young ones with wet hair, loud voices, and quick, weightless movements. I passed them, continuing on through the fragrant pine trees, until an ear-splitting scream sent me running back. I was terrified, convinced someone was drowning or had smashed into a log just beneath the water's surface. I couldn't have been more wrong. As I steadied myself against a tree trunk, almost wheezing from bolting back to the scene, all I saw was a boy swimming back to friends laughing along the shoreline. Everyone was enjoying a pitch-perfect summer day. I stayed in that spot a long time—long enough to believe, not just see, that the boy was unharmed. You have to stop sinking, I reprimanded myself. I couldn't finish the full 2.2-mile circuit that day, but when I did a week later I felt transcendent. It was one of those experiences that have a definitive before and after.

I'm just waiting to be with you someday, I wrote. *Please give me patience.*

The August sun moved directly overhead and sweat dripped down my back, which had gotten stiff against the birch tree. I packed up my journal and drove around for a while before stopping at a circa-1930s motor court. Northwood Cabins was quintessential Adirondacks nostalgia—a crescent-shaped string of squat A-frames with aqua-blue shutters and trim. The cabins looked cozy. I requested the middle one because it seemed the most protected. I may have been ready to hike somewhere I'd never been, but I still craved security.

From the rack of brochures in the Northwood Cabins office, I selected one about a hike up Panther Mountain. According to the brochure, aspiring members of the Catskill Mountain Club were required to summit the mountain twice—at least once in winter—

to be inducted. I decided to give it a shot since the 2,250-foot mountain was billed as a popular and easy one-hour, up-and-down trip. The hike did turn out to be easy, though steep. From the top was a nice view of Piseco Lake, shaped like a slightly bent arm. I felt proud of myself. The mountain may have been small, but I'd scaled it on my own.

Still early enough to get in another hike, I snagged a small nap at the cabin before driving to a trail that another brochure said would lead to a peaceful pond. The trailhead may have been well-marked, but the trail itself clearly had been neglected for years. Some spots were so overgrown I wondered whether I was on a trail at all. By the time I broke out of the woods and reached the pond, it was dusk. Not wanting to get back to the cabin too late, I walked the shore only a few minutes before turning back toward the woods. The only thing before me was a tangle of wood and leaves. I'd lost my bearings. One thicket of trees looked no different than another, no break in the bark an obvious sign of a trail. In the past I simply would've asked Bill, "How do we get out of here?" and he would've figured it out. He was always prepared for unforeseen circumstances, which is why he kept an assortment of emergency kits in his desk drawer. "What could happen to us?" he would ask before every trip, taking into account the terrain and length of time we'd be away. I had one of those kits in my pack, but it was of no use now. I couldn't tweeze or bandage my panic. I prayed and prayed as twice I assumed—incorrectly—that some tamped-down weeds suggested some proximity to the trail. Again and again I blazed my way through the bush only to arrive back at the water. It was getting darker. I cried so hard, my shoulders shook. I told myself to calm down—to be logical, the way Bill had been. Slowing my breath and scanning the woods once again for a telltale break in the tree line, I noticed something I'd missed before, a sliver of land where the bushes gave way to a patch of rough grass. I ran toward the break, my prayers turning into praise when I stepped foot on the worn path. I made it to the car under the last traces of light. Any pride from earlier in the day was a distant memory.

I passed the evening on an old, bouncy metal chair outside the cabin door, eating dinner from a drive-up burger joint down the road and sipping whiskey from a flask. Once drowsy enough for bed I crawled into the sleeping bag I'd spread on top of the sheets. I wanted to drift off while pretending to be camping. I'd be doing the real thing two nights later—for the first time without Bill.

The next day, guided by yet another brochure, I drove to the Whitney Wilderness Area in the town of Long Lake. Mount Frederika was there. Rising 2,180 feet, it was described as an 8.8-mile, easy-to-moderate walk with beautiful views of wetlands, wilderness, and Lake Lila. Not far into the walk, as soon as the trail narrowed and rose up under the trees, I caught a flash of movement several yards to my right. It was a coyote. I stood stock-still. My heart pounded. The brochure hadn't said anything about coyotes. I didn't know what to do. Remain calm and quiet? Wave my arms and yell? Two very different things with, no doubt, very different results. The coyote skedaddled before I landed on an answer. I took one hesitant step, then another, on alert for other wild animals who could be more interested in me than the coyote had been. For a long while, to keep my mind occupied, I looped "Hakuna Matata" from the Lion King CD that had stayed in rotation on my car stereo since Katie's last visit. By the time I reached the overlook above the lake, I'd drained my stash of miniature candy bars and pretzels, my nervous energy quelled by the comforting blend of chocolate and salt. The Lake Lila shoreline, the largest in the entire Adirondack Park, was pristine, probably because it was accessible only from a long dirt road followed by a long walk to the water's edge.

I stared at the water until it moved out of focus.

I had pushed myself. I had made it. I felt like a warrior.

Chapter 22

I left for Maine at 6 a.m. the next morning, on the day Bill would've turned 58. According to my GPS, the quickest way to Maine was through Canada, but scenic roads outranked border traffic. If I snaked along Lake Champlain, I would get to Baxter State Park by dinnertime anyway.

My original plan had been to go from the Adirondacks to New Hampshire. My daughter Michelle's friend Carol lived there, and years earlier she had given me an open-ended invitation to hike with her anytime I was in her neck of the woods. It would have taken four, maybe five, hours to drive to her house—not exactly a neck-of-the-woods calculation—but it seemed a good way to step up my training regimen. When I'd called weeks before, Carol said she wouldn't be home. She and her sister would be finishing up Maine's Hundred-Mile Wilderness, the wildest, most burly stretch of the Appalachian Trail. They planned to end their hike with a 14-mile climb up Mount Katahdin that Carol had done once before. The words fell out of my mouth before I knew they were in my head. Could I come along for the finish? The highest I'd ever climbed was to the top of Blue Mountain in the Adirondacks. Altitude: 3,750 feet. Mount Katahdin was the notorious centerpiece of Maine's Baxter State Park. It stood at 5,268 feet, the highest point in the state. I didn't know Jim too well at this point, but I'd talked with him enough to know he'd made it to the top of Katahdin three times. I had no idea what I was getting myself into, but Carol sounded happy I wanted to join them, which made me feel good. I told her the challenge would be fun because it seemed like the right thing to say. I didn't mention that the trip would rank as the longest I had ever been away from home by myself, and that was counting before Bill's accident.

Through Vermont and into Maine I replayed the previous two days. The memories made me drive slower than the speed limit and knocked me off schedule some, but I didn't care about the time—not until my GPS took me from smooth, single-lane roads into an extensive network of progressively narrow, dirt-covered logging roads. I couldn't make sense of my surroundings and was still more than 20 miles from Baxter State Park. I missed the way my mother and I got around when we traveled through central Maine together in my early 20s. Familiar with the route, she would say, "Turn right by the big tree at the edge of town" or "Turn left when you get to the bridge." Now, not even a satellite-based navigation system was any help. I bumped along for an insufferable hour, turning this way and that, bouncing from confusion to worry to terror. Where am I? Are there going to be any signs? What if I run out of gas and no one finds me for weeks? Soon it would be dark. I cursed my GPS. I didn't care anymore about my plans to meet Carol and her sister by dinner. I just wanted to get back to civilization—alive.

Chapter 23

I bundle up Bill's coat, then lean against Jim for balance to stretch the elastic cuffs of Bill's camouflage pants over my boots. Like the coat, the pants are loose but fortifying.

Feeling secure in Bill's outerwear and with Jim at my side, I walk lead-footed—keenly aware of the effort it takes to inhale—for 45 minutes up the steep route to Lava Tower. "When we go to the summit, Lava Tower will seem only a hill," Yusuf had said last night after dinner. That wisp of a memory makes it even more difficult to breathe. Sue walks in front of us. I zone out on the spines of her boots. At one junction the trail breaks off to the right, leading toward Arrow Glacier Camp on the Western Breach route. That route closed two years ago after three Americans were killed by a rock slide, the result of a melting glacier overhead. The fact that Kilimanjaro has lost 26 percent of its ice cover over the last seven years was just a statistic back in Bloomfield. Here it's an in-our-faces reality with potentially tragic consequences.

Lava Tower is a saw-edged volcanic plug also known as "Shark's Tooth." When it comes into view it is shrouded in mist, jutting skyward like a fist raised in victory. The trail ends here.

Most of the other hikers have already arrived and ditched their packs to pose for photos with their banners.

My head is as foggy as the afternoon. Too winded to go any farther, I wait at the base of the tower while Jim climbs a bit higher and off the trail, taking pictures every few steps. It's too much trouble to reach for my camera. I lean on my trekking poles. Jim comes back just as the mist turns freakishly fast to rain, then sleet. It's hard to see more than two feet away. Conversations stop. I move my tongue to the roof of my mouth, away from chattering teeth.

Phil breaks the stunned silence. "You guys want to head back?"

The decision is unanimous. I walk between Jim and Alison. I haven't gotten to know Alison very well but feel a distinctive bond with her nevertheless, though she has no idea it exists. Her wide-brimmed hat teems with ice pellets.

Headed once more toward the Arrow Glacier Camp junction, Sue loses her footing and goes down hard and fast. "I'm fine," she says quickly, pushing herself up, making it clear she doesn't want sympathy or assistance.

With every step I feel like my own feet are going to slip. There are so many rocks, it's hard to find a place to stab my poles. If I were a gambling woman, I'd put money on a broken bone before we reach camp. Even if I only strain a muscle, what am I going to do? Hobble the rest of the way up the mountain? The precarious descent makes me rabid with both doubt and fear. For more than a year I've wondered whether I will reach the summit. Not once have I thought I'd put myself in real danger.

The fear sweeps me back to one of our earliest JOI hikes, a few months after we formed our group at the Thai restaurant. About a dozen of us were on a trail nestled high in the hills of New York's Ontario County, between Canadice and Honeoye lakes. I was wearing the blue snowshoes I'd ordered two weeks before Bill died. I'd never worn them and had been on snowshoes only a few times in my life, the previous time years before, so it had taken me longer than the others to put them on. Which foot went into which snowshoe? The straps and buckles were a cryptic puzzle. Even after I had given it my best shot, the snowshoes were loose and wobbly, and my poles, refusing to stay locked in place, kept collapsing. We tromped an hour through deep snow before Jack pointed one of his poles toward a steep incline. "The trail loops around there," he said. "Let's take a shortcut and do a little bushwhacking." I'd heard Jack, weeks earlier, say it himself that he was like a racehorse in the woods. Jack and Jim took the lead, maneuvering nimbly around fallen logs into the thick of the forest and down a ravine, as surefooted as if they were walking down the street. It was hard enough for me to be there, a place Bill and I often went cross-country skiing with Michelle, without having to manipulate a ravine in the snow. I took cautious steps and had only one thought, as repetitious as a cricket's chirp—I'm going to kill myself.

Here on Kilimanjaro I try to keep that same chirp at bay as sleet turns to hail. Maybe if I repeat something else I won't plant myself on one of these rocks like a petulant preschooler, refusing to continue on.

I quietly mouth a tried-but-true proverb one circumspect step after another. "A journey of a thousand miles begins with a single step. A journey of a thousand miles begins with a single step."

Rick believes that being in nature reveals our deepest sense of self. "In all types of situations, who you are will come out," he once said. "Do you fight the storms that come or embrace their energy?"

I remind myself that I've navigated long and challenging obstacles before. I beat cancer twice. And what about becoming an engineer? I go through a factual time-lapse: applied for a sales engineering position while working in customer service and attending business school; had no engineering degree so was turned down for the job; followed a recommendation to enroll in an accelerated degree program; quit business school and went part-time at work to attend engineering school full-time; finished school the same month Michelle started college. An onerous process, but when I retired there was only one other woman in the company's 125-person sales force nationwide. All that had to count for something.

I know what comes from zeroing in on what you want, from being tactical. I just need to focus on these single steps.

And continue to pray. *God, keep us all safe.*

The hail wallops harder. My breath becomes more shallow. Camp is still so far away. None of my best attributes—time management, organization—can help me now. What if I wind up with more than a strained muscle and have to stay behind while the rest of the group pushes on? I don't do regret well.

Back to repetition. "Be careful. Be careful. Be careful."

I grip Jim's hand hard to get around and over some of the largest rocks in our way. When I hesitate atop one of the more slippery ones, Jim sets his foot horizontally across the trail in front of me so that I'll slide into it if I slip. I appreciate the gesture. Sue had popped up from her fall fast but she's shorter and, as a result, closer to the ground than I am. I'd land much harder. I try to shift my attention to Jim's chivalrous stance instead of the sharp pain in my knees—a persistent twinge impervious to the Advil I took at lunch for this very reason.

Not until well into our descent does the weather, mercifully, begin to clear, leaving the landscape far below looking as if it has been sifted with flour. Water runs in rivulets off rock ledges as we gradually move into the greener hills of Barranco Valley. By late afternoon, after an 11-hour day on the trail—far from last night's estimate of seven to eight hours—I stagger, sticky and stinky, down the final big slope into Barranco Camp. The camp is in a knoll-studded valley with streams that make it easy for the porters to collect and deliver water quickly. With little wind, the temperature hovers around a relatively warm 40 degrees, an after-storm climatic interlude before night falls. Though the Lemosho and Machame tents are separated, grouped together by trail route, the hikers are all together now. After this afternoon's scare, this brings me more relief than I'd suspected when first reading over our itinerary.

We're at 12,800 feet. Only 200 feet higher than the elevation we'd reached last night. I can accept that we have to "climb high, sleep low," but this—what basically amounts to flat progress over a 24-hour period—is nonsense. A philosophy that had made perfect sense before the climb now just seems cruel. It feels like we're chasing a mirage, the mountaintop closing in then retreating. I had a similar experience on that Alaskan rafting trip with Bill. Rick's brother Randy had been our guide. At the end of one day, with rolling mountains in every direction, Randy pointed to the south and said, "That's where we started this morning." How could that have been possible? It seemed so close yet we had been on the water nearly seven hours. Surely we should've covered more ground. I realized in that moment—a realization I need to keep in mind now—that I'd lost perspective. Distance and control are relative, and beauty can make both irrelevant.

Dinner conversation is minimal. The excited chatter of the first few days is gone. No one cares anymore about table etiquette or formalities. "Will you pass the basket?" has been replaced with "Hand me a piece of bread." Linda Number Two walks into the tent and out again, her stomach unable to handle the smell of ginger soup. She sits in a chair just outside the door with a bowl of rice. We all thought we'd be playing cards or horsing around together after a day's hike, the way we do at home. Rick's optional packing list had suggested bringing a frisbee, football, or kite. I sneer at the thought of such a thing.

The bread is somewhat mashed and starting to taste stale. I'd seen it earlier in the day, stuffed inside a plastic bag tied with twine, on a porter's head. The bag swayed and banged against the box with every agile step. Personally I don't care if there isn't any flavor to savor. At this point food is nothing but fuel for the climb.

We can see Barranco Wall from camp, its trail tiny and barely visible along the menacing 800-foot rock face. The wall was formed long ago by volcanic activity and a massive landslide that caused the mountaintop to collapse inward. There have been less-dramatic collapses since. What are the chances of another eruption happening while we're on the mountain? A less-dramatic collapse is still more than we could survive. As if having to clamber up the wall isn't enough peril to dread on its own.

Turns out I'm not the only one skittish about having to scramble over this monstrosity tomorrow. From one end of the table to the other, hikers ask, "How are we going to scale that thing?" and "Is it even possible?"

More than dubious, I'm edgy. There's nothing to do and nowhere to go to unwind. And my feet are sore.

"I'll just stay right here and you all can get me on your way down," says Linda Number One, whose incapacitating fear of heights is no secret. I give her credit. If I were her, no matter how much I loved to hike or how much I wanted to help obliterate cancer, I don't know that I could be here.

Paul looks at Yusuf. "How difficult is tomorrow going to be?"

"It is a piece of cake," Yusuf answers, his dimples more pronounced than usual. "Like a piece of chocolate cake."

I wish he would give it to us straight. During chemotherapy, nurses told me that when my white blood cell count dropped I would feel tired, weak, maybe short of breath. I would still feel like crap but at least I was prepared to feel like crap. Now it just feels like I've already eaten too much chocolate cake.

Chapter 24

The ranger on duty at the Baxter State Park entrance booth had a booming voice.

"Welcome to Maine! We've been expecting you!"

That second sentence conjured up feelings of guilt for being tardy. Had Carol and her sister reported me as being late? The man knew I was from out of state. What else did he know about me? He exchanged my entrance fee for a park map. "Your friends have checked in. They're about eight miles up the road."

Another eight miles? I thought I was done driving. I'd been lost for the past hour and at a literal crossroad when a small wooden sign pointed the way to the park. Before that I'd stopped to cry and bless myself. I grumbled under my breath while flashing the ranger a polite smile.

The road to the Katahdin Stream campground was curvy and occasionally shored up with sand-covered logs. I wanted nothing more to do with logging roads.

I pulled into the campsite with only a speck of daylight to spare. Carol and Megan waved from a wooden lean-to.

I got out of the car fast. "So good to see you, you have no idea!" I said and slammed the door shut hard as if punishing it.

Carol offered only a light pat on the back before stepping away. "I've been on the trail for several days. You may not want to hug me."

I laughed and shook Megan's hand. "Nice to meet you."

Within the hour all three of us were in our sleeping bags. Carol was reading a book by the light of her headlamp. I was closest to the back wall of the lean-to, built on a wooded bank above the stream the campground was named after. My body was heavy and relaxed against the wooden floor. I missed sleeping outdoors.

"Thanks for letting me camp with you," I whispered. "I haven't done this since Bill died."

"A mouse just walked over my book," Carol said, her voice even-toned. She hadn't even flinched.

I turned onto my side and let the exhaustion close in.

The ground was damp when we awoke, with puddles in spots. I'd slept right through the rain.

We were hoping to hop on Hunt Trail, about a quarter of a mile from the campsite, by 6:30 a.m. That left no time to drive somewhere for coffee—not that I was eager to rely on my navigation system again—so I paired a leftover bagel from the car with water for breakfast.

We arrived on time at the trailhead, near the end of the line for the Appalachian Trail's northbound hikers. The trail was slippery from the night's storm. In Greenland I'd fallen down after a hard rain, my backpack so heavy other hikers had to help me stand back up. I tried my best to avoid a repeat, but the Appalachian terrain was tricky, more closely resembling a steep staircase than a footpath. I was doing more high-stepping than an Irish dancer. Even Carol and Megan with their longer legs had to stretch uneasily to make it up a maze of rocky steps. To scale one boulder two miles into the hike, I steadied myself with my palms and jumped to rest on my chest, earning enough leverage to swing one leg up, then the other, and roll onto my back—pinning my daypack uncomfortably in the process. Carol reached out her hand to help, but not before taking a picture I could almost guarantee would be shared with my daughter.

Soon after, panting and embarrassed, I asked if we could take a break. "I'm really, really sorry. I know I'm slowing you guys down."

"You're doing great," Carol said.

Megan nodded. "We're just glad you're here."

Those were nice things to say, even if they didn't mean them.

For another two miles, winding around the mountain on a wide, gusty ledge, I dug my poles into the spaces between rocks to pull myself along. By the time we broke out of the tree line, I was struggling to catch my breath. The fog was so thick there wasn't even a view. When we saw a man about my age resting on the ground against a rough rock wall, we decided to do the same. In a southern drawl the man told us he'd flown in from Atlanta to help his son finish hiking the Appalachian Trail. He looked me over and I could tell he sympathized. "Ma'am," he said, "I got to this point and knew there was no way I could go on. I just needed to sit here awhile."

Deep down I knew I was in the same boat. Not long before, Carol had warned me that we'd be doing more than mostly high-stepping the rest of the way to the summit. There would be additional mazes, more scrambling. I understood why the indigenous Penobscot Nation coined Mount Katahdin as "The Greatest Mountain." Native American lore holds that the storm god Pamola, a hideous bird-like creature, protects the mountain by killing or devouring mortals who scale to the top. Before leaving home, I thought the words Henry David Thoreau wrote in 1846 after he climbed Katahdin, as if in the voice of the mountain, were simply poetic: "I have never made this soil for thy feet, this air for thy breathing, these rocks for thy neighbors…Why seek me where I have not called thee, and then complain…" Thoreau's words were more than literary jewels—they had given fair warning. I was desperate to bow out. My back hurt and the emergency kit on its own weighed a few pounds. I'd packed a full one, not wanting to take any chances.

Nearly too winded to speak, I gave in. "I just can't do it."

"We understand," Carol said softly. She gestured to my backpack. "If you're going to stay here awhile, put something on or you'll freeze."

I unzipped my pack to retrieve my raincoat, then slowly slipped one arm, then another, into wrinkled sleeves.

"Thanks for everything," I said.

Carol and Megan said short, tender goodbyes, and when it was just me and the man from Atlanta, I unwrapped a granola bar. We sat in silence while I chewed. That this was my third mountain—and a colossal one at that—in four days should've made me proud, even if I hadn't reached the summit. But Kilimanjaro was 14,000 feet higher than Katahdin. A Harvard Medical School article about altitude sickness-related health problems had put mountains the size of Katahdin in the "moderate" range, mountains from 14,000 feet to 18,000 feet in the "very high" range, and mountains with Kilimanjaro's reach in the "extreme" range. I couldn't even become a moderate peakbagger.

"Well, I'm going to head back," the man from Atlanta said, standing up. He adjusted his pack. "Would you like to join me?"

As much as it would've made sense for me to have a companion on the way down, I wasn't ready to move. "I'm going to stay awhile longer, but thanks."

The man nodded. "Good luck to you, ma'am."

Eventually, the ever-threatening sky sent me on my way as well. Acutely aware of my solitude, I treated the descent through the woods as a walking meditation. Step, breath, step, breath. The predictable rhythm kept me company until the path arced to the right and I came face-to-face with a hemlock awash in diffused light. I tilted my head back. The sky was so cloudy, the canopy so thick, how could the beam—warm, regenerating—have forced its way through?

I was sure Bill had something to do with it.

"Thank you," I said aloud.

The rest of the way I was able to concentrate on how far I had come—in so many ways. Definitions for victory and defeat were nebulous. The trails were, by degrees, leading me back to a life I had terribly missed.

The first thing I did when I got home was email Jim, to let him know I had a good time on my trip but failed to reach the Mount Katahdin summit.

"A lot of peakbaggers only concentrate on getting to the top," he responded, "when really the most important thing is the journey."

I couldn't find anything wrong with this man.

Chapter 25

"Goooood morning, Barranco Wall!"

We wake to Rick's version of Robin Williams' booming broadcast greeting in the movie "Good Morning, Vietnam." I would've preferred to rise to the smooth sound of *habari za asubuhi*, the way I've heard the porters greet each other before starting their day's work.

At breakfast, between bites of pale eggs with grilled onions, Barranco Wall is the only topic of conversation except for some grumpy exchanges about running out of Milo. For once no one talks about who snored the loudest or had to get up the most to go to the bathroom. We're all transfixed by the ominous obstacle before us.

"Holy crap, what are we doing?" I whimper to myself later while brushing my teeth, the bristles garbling my words. I close my eyes and pray a familiar refrain. *God, keep us all safe.* I'm too tired to ask for much else. Those five words have worked so far, and it seems like I'm going to need to conserve every ounce of energy just to keep warm. Despite the sleeping bag liner I'd added to my supply list after a recommendation back home, I slept terribly last night—the coldest one yet. I woke up countless times, sitting up with a start at one point to catch my breath. I knew Jim was nearby if I really needed him but I wanted familiar protection. I wanted Bill.

I return my toothbrush to its case and walk in the direction of the toilet tent, only to find it already dismantled. I was hoping to avoid using the only rock at camp large enough to hide behind, given its popularity and odor. Ducking behind the rock won't even assure privacy. The spot is in full view of the Machame camp higher on the knoll. Bearing in mind what Linda Number One had said after I told her about the wayward raincoat incident in Alaska —when Bill got distracted by the flock of ptarmigan—I search for her. It takes only a minute to find her walking out of the food tent.

"Will you hold my raincoat for me?"

She laughs. "You got it."

I grab the coat from my duffel.

"Over here," I say.

Just as I squat, another hiking group sets out from a camp just over the edge of the knoll. Linda Number One moves the raincoat to block their view, inadvertently offering the Machame folks an unobstructed view of their own. Tom, who'd handed out the "IT'S NOT THE ALTITUDE. IT'S THE ATTITUDE" pins on our last training hike, points a finger my way. Jim sits in a chair, not moving a muscle or saying a word. I'll have to remember to tell him he's a smart man.

"Oops, sorry!" Linda Number One says, swiveling side-to-side on her heels, not sure which way to provide cover.

I finish as quickly as I can and zip up my pants without reacting. I'm getting used to this scenario.

About 10 minutes later the Machame group makes its way to Lemosho turf.

I'm grateful no one brings up what just happened.

Instead, a bunch of the Machame hikers tease Jim and me in sing-songy voices. "Jim's going to hike with his girrrl-friend…Jim's going to hike with his girrrl-friend." I love every mocking word.

"I'll catch up soon," Rick says, a solar panel in his hand. "Have to charge the satellite phone."

Catch up? He must still be acclimated from his trip here three weeks ago. He's like one of the porters now, some of them already along Barranco Wall's steep, switchbacked ridges.

Before he leaves, Rick has one last thing to say. "Mohammed is ready!"

The morning haze is burning off, revealing a cerulean sky, and soon enough we are on the precarious wall ourselves. It doesn't take long for the undulating trail, only several feet wide, to become clogged with poky, apprehensive climbers. I tune into the sound of aluminum poles on scree, to heavy breathing. I try not to think about the 500-foot drop-off and instead about how Uhuru Peak is only two days away. After Bill died, I counted the number of days leading me away from him. On the mountain, I've been counting the number of days leading me toward the summit. Only three days away. Only two days away.

Higher up we go.

"My stomach is giving me hell," I overhear Todd saying in front of me. He's the one who called me a badass our first morning on the mountain. "I don't think I've slept a full hour any night since leaving the hotel."

I'm about to offer my sympathy when a voice shouts from even farther behind. "Porter on the left!"

The left? That means I have to step toward the great chasm to my right. Lord knows I don't fear what's on the other side of this life, but what's on the other side of this ledge is another story. There's no straight drop down into the valley below, either. The edge of the mountain slopes and bulges enough for a body to roll, build momentum, then crash into a heap of boulders. Why doesn't the porter pass on the right? I'm sure he could saunter by with his eyes closed. Relying on my poles to keep me stable, I baby-step toward the ledge as the porter, smelling ripe after five days on the trail, whips by, lugging a crate of eggs. The line stays at a standstill, everyone waiting to see whether another porter is in his wake. I take a quick peek into the valley. A person is reclining against a rock next to something on the ground. Must be Rick and his portable charging station. Behind him, a cluster of thin waterfalls drop between cracks in the highest rocks.

"Beautiful, isn't it?" Jim says. I'd asked him to hike just behind me until we clear Barranco Wall.

I can't argue with that. "Just amazing."

The truth is, this is scenery we never would see if not stuck on a ledge on Mount Kilimanjaro. And that's what we are—stuck. Because of the way the trail snakes, I can't tell what's happening up ahead, but word travels back that Linda Number One is immobilized at its narrowest section. She must be at the point where we have to wrap ourselves around an exposed rock spur jutting outward over the trail. We've heard about this specific spot since our early days of training. Not even the summit seems as scary as this does now. I lean into the wall to rest and take deep breaths to slow my own speeding heart rate.

"You holding up?" Jim asks.

I nod. The fear that has lingered since yesterday's descent from Lava Tower is stealthy, creeping from my mind into my trembling limbs, as insidious as dust motes. I feel the way I did in Greenland, when Bill and I climbed a glacier and my foot could press into the ice farther than I thought it should. Could this be like the Western Breach route, where the Americans died? A place where nature shifts and turns fatal? Maybe there are places humans shouldn't go no matter how alluringly billed as life-enhancing tourist destinations.

We hear cheers up ahead. Linda Number One must've made it around the spur. I'm relieved for her, but my relief turns into tension when the line starts moving. My steps again are circumspect. I say a Hail Mary and congratulate myself on planning ahead to have Jim behind me at this particular moment.

When I reach the spur, I put both poles in one hand and turn to face the wall.

"You've got this," Jim says.

I hug the wall, gripping what I can, my body scraping against its barbed edges. No wonder this spot is known as Kissing Rock. All I'd have to do to make things official is pucker my lips, but I'm feeling less than amorous as I take teeny steps to the other side. The other side! I made it to the other side! The energy is intoxicating as Jim swiftly follows and the Karanga Valley—more dirt and lichen, sparser vegetation, and the setting for our final push to the top of Kilimanjaro—comes into view. Over the next hour I'm not even bothered by the hard rain that falls for minutes at a time then suddenly stops, as if set to an automatic timer. I see it only as nourishment for the peanuts growing in the valley below.

When we stop for a snack, Todd breaks away from the group to rest against a striated rock with his eyes closed. I don't see how he could look any more miserable. I feel the need to say something, but he looks like he wants to be left alone.

In a span of minutes we're engulfed by murky clouds. It's difficult to stay oriented.

"We can't see below us, we can't see above us, and there's nothing else alive here," Phil says, pointing with the bottom of his trekking pole at the bleak landscape. "This feels like limbo."

Todd rallies and we continue walking.

We are deep in the high desert now, the ground a moonscape with its path of shale and boulder slabs. Up ahead, lead guide Mohammed stands alone on a rock—left hand pocketed, poker-faced, and with a mystique to match the mountain. I guess that means we're stopping for another break. As the pacesetter, Mohammed knows how to balance our required speed with our need for rest and replenishment.

Two eagles soar. "Bone marrow specialists," Yusuf says. "They drop bones to break them apart and get at the marrow."

I scarf down some peanut-butter-and-cheese crackers. Out of

Chapter 25

earshot, a small group of hikers has gathered around Todd. I want to hear how he's feeling but don't want him to feel crowded so I toe the shale, which sounds like shards of broken glass, and shudder from the cold.

Linda Number Two raises a hand. "I'm not feeling well either," she says.

Rick divides up her things, gives half to Yusuf, and puts her pack over his shoulder.

By the time we've all gone to the bathroom, Todd seems to have perked up somewhat—scarcely, but enough to cross the last two shallow valleys into the barren Karanga Camp. As soon as we reach camp, I walk up to him.

"Glad you were able to make it. I was really worried about you."

"Me too, and thanks."

He looks ready to drop. I tap one of his poles with one of mine. "Hang in there."

We spent over five hours hiking today—longer than expected, no surprise. At nearly 13,400 feet there are no more streams. The porters will have to carry all our water from this point forward. It's oddly warmer than it has been at the other camps.

Tom gives a thumbs-up and looks at the sky, now tranquil once more, steel-blue and cloudless. "One small step for man, one giant leap against cancer."

Kibo is so close. Jim and I pose for a picture in front of the summit, its streaks of snow like ski trails. We can see the short, jagged peaks of Mawenzi, a volcanic cone, about seven miles away. As with most things in these parts, there are legends about why Mawenzi and Kibo, another volcanic cone, no longer are friendly, side-by-side neighbors. One of them, from the Chagga people, says that long ago a poor man looking around the mountain for cattle asked an old woman to help him. Though she pointed him toward a large herd, the man couldn't make the cattle follow him. When he returned to the old woman, she gave him a staff to use. Drive the largest bull and the rest will follow, she told him. Her advice worked, but when the man asked Kibo to move aside so he could drive his cattle home, his request was denied. For a third time the man approached the old woman for help. She said that if he plowed her field she would give him a magical powder to blow upon Kibo's rocks. The man finished the job, took the powder, and did as he was advised. Kibo cracked and split apart from Mawenzi. The man and his cattle went on their way and the two volcanic cones have been separate since. Another legend says Kibo pounded Mawenzi with a pestle, giving Mawenzi its scarred spires. A third legend simply says that Mawenzi is disfigured from his wife Kibo's bite marks. I suppose, just like with the Bible, we all need stories to make sense of our world.

Jim puts his arm around me and points out the soft lines of Mount Meru, about 40 miles away. I can only think about my sleeping bag. The higher we climb, the more rest I require. I peck him on the cheek. "I think I've had it for tonight."

Inside the tent it takes a while to unlace and slip off my boots. My feet hurt. I stroke the sole of each foot with my thumbs before changing into more comfortable clothes and dropping my headlamp into a pants pocket for when it gets dark. Before lying down I position my boots in just the right spot in the tent's vestibule so they won't get wet if it rains. Wet feet cause blisters and I have enough to worry about.

Chapter 26

The ceremonial washing of feet dates back to the Lord's Supper, when Jesus washed the feet of his disciples as a final act of humility and service before being crucified.

Just as with every Holy Thursday, I sat in a chair between the altar and front pew at Saint Bridget's. An aluminum basin, pitcher of lukewarm water, and hand towel were within reach. I always took part in this annual exchange of hospitality three days before Easter, except this Holy Thursday was different. It was the first anniversary of the week Bill died.

The first person to sit across from me was a woman in her 80s. Her bare, bony foot rested in my hand over the basin.

I hesitated.

I never knew about the ritual as a child but had come to love it. Members of the congregation took turns cleaning and being cleaned as a reminder not to put ourselves above anyone else. At first I thought it might be awkward. Although fairly certain the feet wouldn't be half as dirty as they would've been in the ancient Middle East, when sandals were commonly worn on hot, dusty roads, I had plenty of questions. Would people be ticklish? Would I feel embarrassed about having someone wash my feet? Would I remember what to do when it was time to hand the towel to the next person? But instead of being awkward, the tradition had always felt rejuvenating and full of affection.

The woman was waiting on me.

I gave her a counterfeit smile. The Church's dayslong emphasis on death and resurrection was stirring up a cacophony of emotions. I wanted that resurrection for my husband—for him to be given the same chance Jesus had been given to walk the earth once more.

I tipped the pitcher over the woman's foot. The water gently burbled as it hit flesh, then metal, echoing off the high ceilings of the silent church. A brief massage followed, my fingers lightly squeezing the woman's toes before traveling over the rest of her gaunt foot. With the hand towel, I softly pressed cloth to skin.

I hadn't been this intimate with anyone in a long time and I thought about being in bed with Bill, about how our feet used to touch under the covers.

Chapter 27

I have lost a companion on the trail.
The lichen, a steady presence of varying degrees through each microclimate, has vanished this morning. In recent days it had adhered to rocks in a kaleidoscope of colors and patterns before becoming flaky and gray. Yusuf says scientists think Kilimanjaro's largest lichen could be thousands of years old and among the oldest living things on the planet. I know it's just part of the landscape, but I can't help thinking about how lichen isn't a single organism like most other living things. It's a combination of organisms that live together intimately and rely on a partnership to function. That describes all of us on this mountain—living together, relying on each other to get to the top.

We catch beautiful views of Kibo and Mawenzi from multiple angles, all while treading on rock shards that litter the terrain. Some form precarious cairns—stacks of stones—built by previous travelers. I see these often during hikes and frequently add to them. I like searching the ground for a rock that speaks to me, for its curved edges or polished luster, and putting it on the pile. The act connects me in some way to people I will never know.

A German tour group leapfrogs ahead of us, an oversized

umbrella strapped tightly to each hiker's pack. I didn't think to bring an umbrella—it wasn't on Rick's packing list—and am glad I'm not hiking with one. I have enough weight on my back. Waiting on the side of the trail for the last of the Germans to pass, I eye two white-necked ravens on a tall rock, staring in opposite directions as if on watch. Their surveillance comforts me in this strange place.

We walk and walk until we're above the clouds, then we walk some more, taking breaks only briefly to refuel and relieve ourselves. I'm comfortable in my heaviest fleece and gloves. As we reach the last steep stretch before noon, Todd stops to rest on his poles. He looks different now. He looks scared.

"Water break!" Rick bellows.

Todd crumples onto one of the few large rocks around. His eyes are shut tight, and he's visibly struggling to straighten his spine and broaden his chest, presumably for a full breath. Rick is at his side in a blink, unzipping Todd's coat, sticking an ear against his chest. I feel pretty strong in comparison and remember my mother telling me about a woman she met outside a hospital in Rochester. She was there because my father had suffered a brain injury after being kicked in the head by a donkey at a fire department fundraiser. My mother and the woman sat on a bench eating sandwiches and trading stories about their husbands and the surgeries they hoped would return things to normal. The doctors had given my father a decade to live at the most. The other woman, a mother of six, had been told her husband wouldn't see Christmas—only two months away. "From that moment on," my mother said, "I knew that no matter what I was going through, someone else was going through worse."

Rick pulls away. "Your heart is pounding through all these layers. Rest a bit."

My own heart is pounding just thinking about everything that could be wrong with Todd. The books I'd read in preparation for the trip were full of cautionary tales when it came to elevation.

Chapter 27

Tales about acute mountain sickness, high-altitude cerebral edema, high-altitude pulmonary edema. Even with all his climbing experience, how could Rick know if a brain was swelling with fluid or whether lung capillaries were leaking?

I'm sure Todd is thinking about his family—his two kids, his pregnant wife. And probably the summit we plan to reach tomorrow. Ten minutes pass. Rick listens to Todd's heart again. His face conveys there has been no change.

Rick chooses gentle words. "I think this is far enough."

Pointing ahead to where the trail splits, Rick tells Todd that a porter from the Machame route will take him back down the mountain to a camp to rest.

How in the world can Todd keep walking? Is this why Yusuf refers to us as soldiers?

With help from lead guide Mohammed, Todd unfolds into a standing position, though it looks painful to do so. He starts taking slow, measured steps, leaning heavily on his poles. Rick carries Todd's pack to the fork, walks back, and holds out a plastic bag. "Don't short yourselves," he says to the group, "but anything you can spare for Todd, put in here. We'll see him again on the way down."

That's 24 hours from now. So much can—will—happen between now and then. I toss a package of crackers into the jumble of power bars and trail mix and catch up with Todd, who hasn't moved very far. It's hard to say goodbye and move on, especially now, so close to the end.

I touch his arm. "You'll be with us."

Walking away is hard. It feels less like we're leaving Todd in good hands—which I know we are—and more like we're deserting him as we follow the path to the left, out of Karanga Valley and toward the summit. I'm sure Todd is relieved he doesn't have to go any farther, but it can't be easy watching us disappear around the bend. My heart feels as heavy as my pack.

A steady breeze blows a light mix of snow and rain. Swirling clouds intermittently reveal the long gravelly slope of the summit cone ahead. I have to stop frequently to lean on my poles, my rubbery legs struggling to keep pace, my knees screaming for more Advil. By the afternoon, it's hard to keep my footing on the stony trail so I stare at my feet. It would take too much work to lift my head anyway. My pack doesn't hold anything more than it did earlier but now feels oppressive.

When the breeze finally lets up and the sun peeks through the slate sky, I feel slightly hopeful but mostly find the thin air and frigid weather intimidating— even after layering on Bill's coat. When we come to another split in the trail, the Lemosho group has to part company with the Machame group one more time, temporarily. The Machame hikers will head to Barafu Camp, where most people who climb Kilimanjaro try to sleep for a few hours before attempting to summit. The Lemosho gang will camp on a small flat spot nearly 500 vertical feet above Barafu Camp. Rick told us there would be less wind and fewer people there. More important, at nearly 15,700 feet, it is one hour closer to Stella Point, on the edge of the Kibo crater's rim and one of three official summit points. From there we can decide whether to continue on another 600 feet to Uhuru Peak, the highest point on the mountain. The plan to leave from Barafu Camp gives us a huge advantage in the wee hours of the morning, when the sky is pitch black and many hikers feel depleted even before taking their first step. If we start our last walk toward the summit just after midnight, when the trail is frozen, the journey will be easier—and, if timed right, will allow us to reach the rim at sunrise.

"Good luck," I tell Jim. I lean into him, want to stay there, but a guide briskly shepherds me along to keep up with the rest of the Lemosho group.

Climbing higher than the Machame group on summit night

had always sounded good in theory. But on this next stretch, feeling clumsy scaling the last steep slope into camp, it seems absolutely necessary. Collecting all the air I can, I exhale a shallow sigh of relief that we don't have to do this part in the dark. I'm even more thankful for the view. The Kibo glacier gleams in the late-afternoon sun, wholly resplendent, its pillars of frozen water like cathedrals.

I'm almost to my tent when the porters stream out of their own tents to welcome us with a traditional dance and song:

Kilimanjaro, Kilimanjaro,
Kilimanjaro, mlima mrefu sana.
Na Mawenzi, na Mawenzi,
Na Mawenzi, mlima mrefu sana.
Ewe nya, ewe nya,
Ewe nya, mbona saninzungukaa.

Kilimanjaro, Kilimanjaro,
Kilimanjaro, very tall mountain.
And Mawenzi, and Mawenzi,
And Mawenzi, long mountain journey.
Oh my, oh my,
Why don't you go around me?

My limp limbs go limper still as I take in the sweet surprise. I glance from one porter to another, feeling appreciation for their smiles, their vibrant knit hats, how happy they appear to be as they gather us together to dance. With a surge of energy, coming from I don't know where, I drop my pack, throw my hands in the air, and snap my fingers. My feet, spent from the day's hike, barely move.

I look from the Africans clapping and hopping from one foot to the other, to Mawenzi and Kibo, both peaks blanketed with snow.

My eyes pool. Numerous rounds later the porters stop and we applaud.

Bending my knees to pick up my pack, I look around for my green plastic sack and tent, pitched on a windswept ridge. Inside the tent I move slower than ever through my routine. Someone calls out "Tea and popcorn!" but the only thing on my agenda is bundling up in my sleeping bag. I scooch inside the bag, burying my face to block out the light. How can I possibly give my body enough rest for the big night ahead?

The next thing I know—other than that I don't want to move—Sue is calling me to the food tent for dinner. I don't even remember falling asleep.

Dinner is simple. Potato soup and spaghetti with meat sauce, both laden with fortifying carbohydrates for this last stretch up the mountain. We are a motley crew in varying stages of misery and gastrointestinal distress. My stomach wants to stage a revolt but the toilet is taken. I tell myself not to start with the questions but can't help it. What if I have diarrhea on the trail—or worse? What if I have to be sent down like Todd? Does Jim even think about things like this?

"Remember to sleep in the clothes you're wearing for the summit tonight," Rick says. "You want to save time and energy once the wake-up call comes. That'll be in four hours, so finish up and try to get some sleep."

He doesn't have to tell me twice.

This is the only time on the mountain Yusuf sets an alarm.

Someone is calling for us to get ready for the final ascent. Again, I must've fallen asleep fast. To my surprise I wake easily and well-rested, though more worries set in. Will I be warm enough? Will my headlamp produce enough light? Will I be able to say I made it?

Chapter 27

Sue is checking her oxygen level. On her face, a mixture of dejection and anxiety.

"You okay?" I ask.

"Seventy-seven."

I've learned on this trip that a normal reading at sea level is at least 95. At home she would be admitted to the emergency room for respiratory distress.

She shrugs. "Onward."

I give her an encouraging smile and pull on layer upon layer upon layer. My hands are fatigued and moving in slow motion by the time I finish tying my boots. The next time I touch these shoelaces, the drama will be over.

The air outside is bone-chilling cold. There's a new dusting of snow on the ground but the stars are brilliant, the well-defined glow of the Milky Way seemingly so accessible at this altitude. Rick and a few hikers are in a huddle, staring up at the galaxy's hazy swirl. I walk over.

"You can't miss being humbled," Rick says. "These are very spiritual places. When you stand in them, if you're open to it, you experience life on a different plane."

Kevin points to what looks like a star steadily moving across the sky. "That could be the International Space Station. I saw it once from my friend Lenny's house. We use his telescope and tracking maps to look for satellites, planets, comets. It's what nerds do at night."

"Look this way," Rick says. He's pointing in the other direction, over the edge of the mountain. "That's Moshi down there."

Search lights from a popular nightclub reach upward from more than 12,000 feet below. Weaker lights flicker from other towns spread out in small patches. How far away everything looks. How far we've come.

"It's warm down there," Rick says. "Mosquitoes are carrying malaria. I prefer the cold."

I carefully stretch for a few minutes before ducking into the food tent for a cookie and sip of tea, careful not to drink any more than that to head off the urge to urinate on a steep incline in the dark. Paul and Linda Number Two are lamenting how little sleep they got. They were unable to tune out the wind—I can't imagine what the wind speed was at the more exposed Barafu Camp below us—and a loud German in the adjoining camp. I feel lucky to have zonked out with no problem.

There's no time for more than a sip of tea anyway.

Rick hollers from outside the tent. "Double-check your gear and let's get going!" The command sends a chill through me that the air can't match. There is no more time to think about what might happen on summit night. We are about to find out.

I return to my tent to gather my things and emerge looking ready for battle.

Rick points to Kim's hoop earrings. "You have to take those off," he says. "They're going to freeze to the side of your face."

I can't tell whether he's joking.

A startling cry comes from the toilet tent. Rick sprints into the dark, followed by a few porters. I stare up at the sky and wait, nerves piling on top of nerves. Word filters back that one of the hikers didn't make it to the bucket in time and needs help cleaning up and getting dressed again. After spinning my head to see who's missing, my stomach drops.

Sue.

I can't imagine what she's feeling or how Rick deals with the pressure that comes with this job—how he needs to make one split decision after another to keep everyone safe.

Even the strongest are floundering.

"It took me 20 minutes to tie my shoes," Paul says.

I lightly bump Linda Number Two's hiking boot with my own. "How are you feeling?"

"I'm anxious," she says. "Worried I won't be warm enough, worried that my headache will be debilitating. But it's no longer in my hands. I'll do my best."

Chapter 27

Paul unzips his coat partway and pulls out his water bottle, stuffed inside a wool sock. When Rick said we should keep our water bottle on summit night as close to our bodies as we can, it never occurred to me to wear it. Mine is in an insulated carrier in my pack. Why aren't I following directions on what is certain to be one of the hardest nights of my life? Lead guide Mohammed takes his place. Time has always moved tremendously slow on the mountain, and now all I can picture are the hands of a clock spinning in accelerated motion. There's nothing I can do about the water bottle now.

We snap on our packs and zip up our gaiters that are supposed to keep small stones from working their way into our boots on the quicker descent. I take my place in line, nervous and queasy.

Out of the corner of my eye I see Rick walk up to Yusuf. I train my ear on him. He says Sue will be joining us in a moment. She's downing two medications for traveler's diarrhea. I say a silent prayer of thanks.

"So now…" Yusuf says loudly.

No one needs him to finish his sentence. We all file into line, knowing Mohammed is ready. This much has been drilled into us.

So this is why Yusuf calls us soldiers.

"In seven hours you'll be feeling a lot better," Rick says. "Listen to your body. Tell your guides how you're doing. You'll make it."

Chapter 28

"Maybe it's God's sense of humor that today's gospel reading is about Jesus being transfigured on the mountain," Father John's voice bellowed from the pulpit.

I was at St. Matthew Catholic Church for the first time. Several JOI members belonged to the church, and about one-third of the group was gathered on the last Sunday before our departure for Tanzania to share in worship and prayer and receive a special blessing from the congregation.

Father John preached that through hardship and the gift of grace, our own transformations happen. "One thing is for sure," he said of those of us going to Kilimanjaro. "Like Peter, James, and John, they will not come down the mountain the same people they were when they went up."

How would I be affected? Would I come down the mountain more open to scriptural teachings I don't always understand? Would I become more open in other ways?

After the homily, Sue, who had rarely set foot in a Catholic church, went to the pulpit to read—first in Hebrew, then in English—a popular Jewish prayer often recited when appealing for a safe journey:

Chapter 28

May it be your will, our God and God of our ancestors,
that You lead us in peace and help us reach our destination
safely, joyfully, and peacefully.
May You protect us on our leaving and on our return,
and rescue us from any harm,
and may You bless the work of our hands,
and may our deeds merit honor for You.
Praise to You, Adonai, Protector of Israel.

I listened to the words carefully, taking special note of the lines about safely reaching a destination and the desire to be protected and blessed. They spoke to my travels through widowhood and offered me footing for my journey to Africa.

I'd recently run into a woman who came to Saint Bridget's every now and then. We'd first spoken two years before at the cemetery where Bill was buried. She'd walked up without introduction and with tears in her eyes. I took one look at her and stopped dusting grass clippings off the base of Bill's heart-shaped headstone. She said she was visiting her husband's grave and that cancer had taken him fast a few months back. She didn't know what to do without him. I told her I was sorry for what she was going through. The woman broke down and repeated herself as the bell tower chimed, the way it always did on the hour. "It's a difficult time," I said. The woman sobbed heavily and told her story one more time before thanking me for my time and leaving. This last time we'd crossed paths was at the church's annual chicken-and-biscuit dinner. Unfortunately, the woman's pain was as fresh as it had been at the cemetery as she reminisced about the years she and her husband attended the dinners. I wanted to say that I hadn't forgotten about Bill and that I would never forget about Bill, but that it wouldn't do me or the people around me any good to mourn with such sadness for the rest of my life. Instead I kept quiet and nodded, knowing that some people have to accept reality on their own terms, and that some need answers before they can move on—even if the answers won't ever be clear. For me that interaction underscored the slow, gradual process I'd gone through since the accident. It had offered a palpable awareness that time heals. I was so thankful I wasn't lost. I was incredibly sad, but not lost.

When Sue finished her reading, Father John invited our entire hiking group to stand before the congregation for the blessing. Sidestepping out of the pew, I thought about how I'd been blessed by a priest each time I had cancer, anointed with a sacramental oil for peace, strength, and the courage to endure. While we most certainly would need those three things on the mountain, such appeals for protection were usually reserved for the weak, helpless, or terminally ill.

On the pulpit, facing all those people with their serious faces and outstretched fingers, a question persisted.

What did we get ourselves into that we had to be blessed?

Chapter 29

We head upward at our slowest pace yet. The trail twinkles with ice crystals as we walk between two glaciers toward Kibo's rim. For this last part of the trek—the summit push—seven more Africans have joined us, some without gloves or flashlights.

I walk behind Sue, who seems to be holding up pretty well. Rick stays close by. "Click off your headlamp just before sunrise," he says. "You'll see the silhouette of the glacier."

He's talking about the Furtwängler Glacier, now a mere remnant of the ice cap that once covered the mountain. I read somewhere that there used to be enough ice on the summit to cover half of Manhattan, and what's left now would cover only half of Central Park. Rick once said this part of the trip is like being in a small tunnel separated from the rest of the world—a precious mix of feeling both vulnerable and at peace for a brief period of the night. Right now I can't believe anything about this night will be brief.

My pace is methodical, the way I moved through my first days as a widow when everything felt protracted. I wonder how Jim is doing. Are his feet cold? Did he sleep well? Did he sleep at all?

If someone talks it's only to share a scant observation. Otherwise, the glacial air is cut only by the consistent crunch of footsteps and the occasional cough.

We've only been walking about a half hour when Sue veers toward a rock on the side of the trail and sits down.

I stop. "Are you okay?"

Rick walks up and squats to get a good look at her face. "Do you feel sick again?"

"Yeah." Sue pushes herself up but can't stand straight. She looks half asleep.

Rick holds out his arms to steady her. "Do you feel weak?"

"Yeah."

Rick motions for me to keep going, but I don't want to leave Sue. He signals for a porter to take her back to camp and waves his arm at me again. My feet follow his instructions, but I'm livid—at Rick for making me continue on by myself and at the situation itself. Sue worked as hard as anyone to be here. This isn't fair—to either of us.

In seconds I'm swept into familiar territory—abandoned without warning. I'm not sure I can make it without Sue. In my mind an aerial view shows me tiny and alone on the mountain. I hear my nephew's voice. He'd watched nervously as I wrangled a canoe onto the top of my car last summer. "Are you sure you can do it, Aunt B?" he asked during the flailing. I needed to prove that I could. "You guys aren't going to be here all the time," I answered, feeling like a toddler learning to walk without grasping for an adult's outstretched hand. Trying to contain my frustration over Sue's departure, I stab the trail with my trekking poles, but the effort only zaps me of energy I desperately need for the rest of the climb.

I look at the sky, the sliver of moon.

Bill, stay with me. I pull the hood of his coat closer around my face and use his words, the ones I found in his journal, to keep him close. "Lord, show me and teach me your ways. Direct me to your truth, for you are God, my Savior."

I appeal to the family members I've lost, starting with my brother, who worshipped Thoreau—he quoted him profusely—and would have loved this mountain. Jerry was a fighter. We hiked together the weekend before his first chemotherapy treatment. It was autumn and the leaves on the ground were wet. Jerry slipped and fell on a rock so hard he could barely walk afterward. Determined not to let an injury interrupt his treatment, he refused to see a doctor about the pain from the fall. Later that week, once the chemotherapy drugs were in his veins, he said, "By the way, you guys may want to check out something else." Tests showed he had a cracked hip. I appeal to my mom, and to both my grandmothers—all three outlived their husbands as well. When my father died, I thought I knew what my mother was going through. I know better now.

I think of Sister Dorothy and all the people back home praying for me. They're all doing their job. I must do mine.

Every hour, about every 500 feet, we pause for a 90-second water break. Once at 17,000 feet, nearly halfway through the night's march to Stella Point, we earn a slightly lengthier respite—this time with tea behind a long row of boulders, protected from the wind. We drink from glass mugs. Again, I marvel at how careful the porters have to be as they hustle up and down the mountain.

No one says a word. Leaning against the rock, I close my eyes to focus on the hot liquid coating my throat. Even as the altitude's low humidity and air pressure are sucking moisture from my skin and lungs faster than usual, I allow myself only a few sips of tea, still mindful of my bladder. My peanut-butter-and-cheese crackers, for once, aren't very satisfying. I want an energy bar instead but they're frozen, just like my feet are starting to feel. So much for toe warmers. I'd worry about frostbite but don't have the strength.

Sadly, this respite seems to fly by as fast as the others. The Africans swoop up the mugs and usher us to our feet. They have to make sure we don't get too cold. Hypothermia is a real risk at this altitude and a lot can change in a matter of minutes—something I understand once back on the trail.

All of a sudden I can't trust my eyes. The trail drops off at a precipitous angle to the right, requiring me to lean severely to the left to avoid a ledge that didn't exist a second ago. Does it even exist now?

One rock after another blocks my path, only to disappear as I reach each one.

I must be hallucinating.

I'm starting to think Yusuf's father may be on to something. Are we on an unattainable mission to reach God? The break we took for tea, only minutes ago, feels like yesterday. A porter up ahead croons an African lullaby. Hikers pass, though I can't distinguish any of them, all bundled up in the dark.

I stop with some other Lemosho laggers to rest my head on my poles, keeping my lips apart to breathe. The air against the back of my throat feels like cold storage. Far ahead the volcano rim beckons, barely lit by the headlamps of the heartier. I can't tell if I'm dreaming.

"Bonnie?"

It takes a lot of energy to look up. My head has taken on the weight of an overstuffed suitcase. Yusuf and Rick appear out of the inky air. They look concerned.

Rick waves me toward him. "What are you doing here? We need to get you with the others."

It takes an enormous amount of effort to find my voice. It feels buried under my boots. "Isn't this…our…group?"

Rick shakes his head. "Are you okay?"

That's a good question. I have one of my own. Am I ridiculous to think that I can climb the world's tallest free-standing mountain? I look into his eyes and convince myself they're full of skepticism. I'm scared Rick is going to order me to turn around and that the past 14 months of training will end here, only a few hundred feet from the summit. I can't let that happen. All those hours building up endurance, all those sore muscles, all those prayers from supporters back home can't be for nothing. I shut my eyes. Trying to think of what to say next but unable to parse my thoughts, I buy time with a nip from my water bottle, though the inside is mostly ice.

I replay Rick's question and realize how I must look to him. I need to convince both men that there is nowhere for me to go at this point but up.

"I'm okay, but...could someone...please...carry my pack?"

What comes next is a visual cocktail of the past and present. One minute I'm using every ounce of strength to set my foot on solid ground, the next I'm fully inside a memory.

Recovering from a chemo session. Almost done reading the entire Old Testament and considering doing it over, though I'd skip Numbers. Too mundane. It takes forever to get from the living room recliner to the bathroom. I think about every step and then, once through the doorway, congratulate myself with a vivacious "Great job!" When I make it back to the recliner I pick up my journal. "In this moment," I write, "I can thank God for my feet continuing to give me their support. Not everyone has this gift."

My feet have lost all sensation. In my head I practice "Moonlight Sonata" and preludes by Bach and Chopin. My insides quake. They get this way sometimes when I'm overly tired, ever since my first round of cancer treatments. After two-and-a-half weeks of radiation, I would come home bone-tired from work—where conversations about equations and electrical principles had become taxing—and lie down to recover, waiting for the quivering to subside. Two months after the treatments were over, when I still hadn't bounced back, I thought about taking some time off, though never did. My boss worried I wasn't taking care of myself.

I have no idea whether I'm taking care of myself now. Maybe I pushed on when I should've turned back.

Test driving a canoe, alone on Irondequoit Bay. The canoe drifts this way, then that way. The waves are stubborn, their points like elf hats. A lanky salesboy watches from the shore about 50 yards away. I have no idea how to steer the canoe. Bill and I used to have a system. I would navigate from the stern, he would provide the power up front. Now that he's not around I feel helpless—even in a single-person canoe much smaller than the heavy, foam-padded metal one that has leaned, untouched, against the side of our shed since the accident. Only 15 minutes out I am ready to quit but can't seem to make it back to the dock. I paddle strenuously against the wind but move only inches toward land before getting caught in a cluster of cattails.

I hover the paddle over the water. The wind is unforgiving as it whips over the bay. I look self-consciously at the salesboy, who is keeping his eyes on me from under his baseball cap. He's probably in high school. I bet he could get unstuck without a struggle.

I bury the impulse to shout for him. Arms burning, I paddle and paddle until I break free.

Time bends. Yards of progress feel like miles. For hours I trudge ahead in a hypnotic trance, my silhouette a wilted flower, the visions unrelenting. My stomach roils as I lurch ahead, and my chest works harder to accommodate an oxygen level only about half the amount found at sea level. At this altitude the smallest physical pains take on cosmic proportions.

If Bill were here, he would be handling this like a champ. He had a high tolerance for pain. One summer, tramping toward an ice cap above the Arctic Circle, he slipped on a scree-covered ridge and tore his meniscus. From then on, keeping pace with the group must have been excruciating—though he was able to make an astoundingly quick exit from the tent one evening to watch a line of women cross the hip-deep river in their bras and panties, their clothes strapped to packs held overhead. Bill's orthoscopic surgeon later said the cartilage looked frayed as a lace curtain. Another time he waited three days to see a doctor for stomach pains that turned out to be a ruptured appendix.

I, on the other hand, have never felt more defenseless. I want a whiskey. I want to survive.

Taking one of Rick's overnight survival courses with Bill. We each are allowed only the clothes on our backs, a garbage bag, and a granola bar, though the granola bar comes with a caveat—no consumption until bedtime. Bill's the one who wants to do this. I won't go so far as to call him a survivalist, but he does like to be obsessively prepared. We could live a long time on the food he stockpiles in our cupboards. He learned to hoard provisions from his grandmother, who once showed me how to make schnitzel out of anything so long as there was an egg and some flour handy.

When we took an hourslong survival course with Rick a few years ago, Bill had been the only participant able to start a fire in a muddy parking lot—a feat he gloated about for years. This particular course is going to take way more commitment. Rick had made it clear when we registered that some people will find it extremely hard to outlast the night. They're not used to the quiet. After the sun sets it's just them, the darkness, and the anxiety that comes from not having anything to do but focus on the moment. Plus it will be really cold. These classes are purposely planned for nights when temperatures easily drop into the 30s. It takes guts to sleep outdoors in such weather without a tent or sleeping bag. Rick had emphasized that we'll have no choice but to adapt, and that discomfort is a great motivator. "There's an illusion of control in the man-made world," *he told us,* "but nature rips that away and gives you all the clarity you need."

It takes about an hour to walk past overgrown homesteads and fences to Rick's chosen spot in an old-growth forest. We spend much of the first day building a lean-to with small branches and sticks and gathering food for the night—walnuts, hickory nuts, acorns, crayfish. We cook meager meals over a roaring campfire and make tea from wild mint and stream water. After dinner, Rick and an assistant dig a trench, fill it with coals from the fire, and cover the coals with a thick layer of dirt. This is where the assistant will sleep. We take turns lying on the fresh mound. I set myself down gingerly, not knowing what to expect. My muscles relax against the warm earth. If this is what surviving in the wild feels like, bring it on.

Once the fire dies down, Bill and I retreat to our lean-to and make another, smaller fire. Before long Bill spreads his garbage bag on a cushion of leaves and promptly falls asleep. I stare at the fire and shiver, wishing I could forget about the assistant's accommodations. I contemplate whether to lie down on the bare ground and use my bag as a blanket, then decide it's too cold for rest. My remaining options are limited. I can listen to my teeth chatter or stoke the fire. Either way I'll be tired in the morning, so I choose to stoke the fire between unsatisfying catnaps.

By 5 a.m. I've run out of sticks to fuel the flames. I look at the lean-to, eyeing our primitive handiwork for kindling. I manage to extract a few sticks without a problem before one lands with a smack on Bill's stomach. He sits up with a start. I'm too tired to care that he's been shaken from a deep sleep.

"Oh, not to worry." My voice is calm. "I'm just tearing the house apart."

Bill has no trouble falling back asleep. I stoke the embers to the echo of his snores. We all survive in our own ways.

The past feels more present than the present.

I force myself to walk, each step ungainly, the tips of my boots dragging over the frozen dirt. I give myself instructions. Left foot,

Chapter 29 191

follow the right foot. Right foot, follow the left foot. My eyes are slits. My nose drips. My teeth are filmy. I hadn't thought about brushing them before we left since nobody had shown up with water basins. I am one implausible, uniform ache, little more than raspy breath and hampered motion.

But unlike when I had cancer, I know this pain is finite.

The first shades of light illuminate Kibo.

Chapter 30

I finally reach the rim at Stella Point, the ground suddenly and deliciously flat. The sun is an amorphous ball of fire against bright bands of tangerine and rust.

"You're one step closer to Uhuru Peak!" Rick says, his arms spread wide.

I can see the curvature of the earth.

So this is what the edge of the world feels like. This is something I'd expect to read about in *National Geographic*, not see with my own eyes. The warped horizon reminds me of car rides in the country with Sister Dorothy, who likes to look over the fields and say, "And God fills that space."

Kevin is curled over a large rock, dry heaving. He has lost at least 10 pounds since the trailhead.

Should I sit down? Take a short break?

Kevin looks up. "Are you going…the rest of the way?"

How should I answer? Bill would know what to do. Even if he didn't know he would pretend he knew, because he was usually right in the end.

I shrug and sit on another rock. I barely made it to the rim so maybe pushing on in my condition would be greedy. My father always told me to trust my instincts, but they're not taking a stand in either direction. My oldest sister always said she had two dads—the one before the donkey kicked him in the head and the one after. Since I was only three months old when that happened, I only knew the one after. The one who was sort of nervous, not great with balance, and barely drove. He worked at the grocery store stocking shelves and stamping prices on the tops of tin cans. I was 11 or 12 when he got promoted to cashier. Going to Buffalo two hours away for the cashier training was a big deal, and because of his brain injury, navigating a bus route to get there was an even bigger deal. Our family celebrated with a special dinner the night before he left. Liver, bacon, and onions. It was the sense of accomplishment—not anyone else's definition of success—that mattered. A good lesson but only of use in this moment on Kilimanjaro if I feel accomplished. And I don't. On training hikes back home, we had all talked about how this trip wasn't about getting to the top of this beast of a mountain but about the journey along the way. That had always sounded like a line straight out of some reality TV show. Did we really mean it? Did I?

I look in the direction of Uhuru Peak. That's where people who summit take their celebratory pictures, waving and striking muscle poses in front of a wooden sign covered with tattered prayer flags. Another 600 feet—less than the length of two football fields. If only the trail were as flat.

I need to answer Kevin, who has just finished another round of dry heaves.

"Yeah, I think so."

Rick walks over to another climber. I can't make out who it is, but I hear him say "corneal edema" and call for a porter to assist with a descent. I've never heard of that condition before but I know it has to do with the eye. Whatever corneal edema is, I hope it's temporary.

I'm not ready to stop—surrender?—but I can't fathom how to keep moving forward. In that respect I imagine I'd been on a rim of sorts after Bill's death, except the situation had been in reverse. Back then I wasn't ready to keep moving forward but was unable to stop. Every day were countless small decisions that had to be made, and with or without my blessing, they ultimately morphed into progress.

Rick's voice is in my head again, this time because of something he said years ago. "We bring to the mountain whatever is in us."

What do those words mean for me? Is getting to Uhuru Peak about ego or something else? And what about the banner in my pack? Other people are relying on me to bring their messages to the top of the mountain, aren't they? How can my brain, at this altitude, possibly process answers to all these questions?

Rick walks over.

"How…long…to…the…top?" I have to inhale between each laborious word.

"About an hour," he says. His tone makes me think, again, if he's wondering whether I have the stamina to make it.

Only about 65 percent of those who attempt to reach Uhuru Peak each year actually do, and I'm sure a lot of them are much younger.

The idea of pressing on is as terrifying as it is tempting, but I have to keep going. I want to summit as much as I don't want to give Rick the chance to say anything else—equal parts primordial urge and act of defiance.

It takes longer than it should to stand up but I take one step, then another, then another, leaving behind any hesitation in a string of frosty footprints. I'm moving even slower than before. I take only three or four steps in a row before stopping to rest my head on my poles. No need for *pole, pole* reminders now. The pace is grueling regardless. My heart is in a race for Olympic gold.

Yusuf takes my arm. "You are almost there."

"You'll…come…with me?"

"Of course. We can do this."

Chapter 30

I try to milk the energy from each short burst of breath—convinced I'll make it with every inhale, skeptical on every exhale. I think of how Rick once spent three days cleaning a Swiss Army knife with a toothpick while waiting to be rescued from a plane crash in the Arctic. Each tiny piece of dirt he excavated gave him a feeling of success. I start counting each inhale as a tiny triumph. During one lift of the head to look at something other than the ground, I catch a flash of orange among the jagged rocks in the distance. Jim's bright coat. He must be on his way down from the summit already. I wish I could run toward him.

I give Yusuf's arm a squeeze. "I have...to stop...and...say hi."

"No problem," Yusuf says. "We have time."

At first it seems he's putting me at ease, letting me know I don't need to feel rushed when saying hello because we can arrive at the summit at my own pace. It soon becomes clear, when the orange coat seems fixed in space up ahead, what he really means. We have a lot of time before Jim and I finally reach each other.

I have no idea how long it takes, but eventually I can make out that Jim is with Jack and some of the other Machame hikers. When he's close enough to touch, I collapse into him. He absorbs my weight without budging. That security is what I need.

"Congratulations," I say through tears into his chest.

Jim's voice is faint, muffled by the hood of Bill's thick coat. "Congratulations to you too."

Yusuf puts his arm through mine for the final, windy ascent.

I pull away from Jim by degrees and wave feebly to the others.

"See you soon," he says.

We are so close to the end that our view is mostly sky, along with patches of snow and dirt and scattered rocks. Trying not to think about my overworked muscles and joints, I concentrate on the absurd notion that the "Roof of Africa" is only a short distance away. All the training and all the uncertainty feels far away now, as far away as Bloomfield.

I'm really doing this, I tell Bill.

"Congratulations!" The words on the sign are carved in English. "You are now at Uhuru Peak, Tanzania, 5,895 M. AMSL. Africa's Highest Point. World's Highest Free-Standing Mountain. One of World's Largest Volcanoes. Welcome."

Yusuf pats my back. "You made it."

I slowly turn my head to take in the southern lip of Kibo. A vertical ice wall—close enough to walk to, though none of us will be attempting to do so—marks the edge of the Furtwängler Glacier, a glimmering mixture of blue, white, and cream.

At 19,341 feet above sea level, above expansive, frothy clouds, I should feel small but I don't. I feel enormous and powerful and deserving of the poet Rumi's words: "You are not a drop in the ocean. You are the entire ocean in a drop."

A few people I don't know are wandering around, some of them likely from the group I joined earlier this morning, back when the thought of me standing here seemed virtually improbable. Some JOI hikers are jockeying for position in front of the sign to pose for pictures with their banners. Rick, with several cameras slung over his shoulders, seems to have become the official photographer. Off to the side with her husband, Kim removes a glove and taps a pill bottle against her palm. The wind carries away her father's ashes, sparkling in the sunlight.

I visualize my own banner and think about all those names and the memories linked to them. About what I wrote to Bill:

*It is your strength
that will carry me.*

Where I'm standing may not be heaven, like the Pare people believe, but it's the closest I've been able to get to Bill, physically at least, since he died. Raw as an open wound, I hang my head and sob.

Chapter 30

Yusuf moves a few feet away—far enough to give me space, close enough to be available. A few minutes later, still sniffling, I hold out my camera.

"Will you take my picture?" I sound sloshed, but now that I'm done walking uphill I can string the words together without too much exertion. We wait for an opening and walk over to the sign. I grip a post and give the lens a weary, satisfied smile.

Rick holds up his satellite phone. "Who wants to record the group's final audio post?"

"I will!" The words come out before I can think about them. I walk over to him, each step easier than the last from the newfound adrenaline and gift of flatter ground.

Rick dials and hands me the phone.

"Hi, this is Bonnie, and I am right now standing at the top of Mount Kilimanjaro." I mumble the start of a second sentence but have to stop to breathe. That first one had been my longest uninterrupted speaking streak in recent memory. I wish I'd been able to rehearse. "It's actually pretty hard, I think, for any of us to be up here this morning without the emotions…We all came up here for such a very special reason…We brought lots of names, lots of people, lots of memories up here with us. I think…"

I pause again to let the tears flow.

"During the past few days all of us would admit…this is a metaphor for our lives. We can do anything we put our minds to… one step at a time."

My eyes turn from Rick to the sky, the glacier, the volcanic landscape. Awe is everywhere.

I take a deep breath. "We're having a wonderful time…This is a beautiful part of the world…Love to everybody."

I hand the phone back to Rick, then walk away to be alone.

Alone. I actually want to be alone. I feel an unburdening of grief, confusion, indecision. With that audio post I have just proven —with concrete, physical evidence, to myself and the rest of the world—that I am inexorably and vehemently alive.

The initial descent is like a vigorous exhale, a barely controlled slide atop scree, the dusty trail warmed by the sun. The wind sweeps the smallest hikers down the mountain like paper bags.

"Going down is the best medicine," Rick says.

I should be cautious. Coming off Katahdin, feeling cocky for having attempted to summit in the first place, I'd laughed just before my foot slipped on the stone steps at the trailhead. I landed flat on my back, as flat as possible with my pack on—my second time in as many hours but who was counting? I don't want a repeat performance.

We're following the Mweka route on our return to camp, where we'll get to rest and snag a quick bite before continuing on to our very last campsite. With our backs to Uhuru Peak, it gets easier by the minute to take in oxygen. This means we can cover more ground in less time. Under an intensifying morning sun I work up a sweat until I feel spiked-fever hot and have to tear off my coat.

I have no idea how, after reaching Uhuru Peak, we're able to walk another three hours to camp—even if it *is* all downhill—but we do. I'm one of the last to arrive, indisputably exhilarated. There's only one problem. I'm also exhausted, and just a few steps from my tent my feet refuse to carry me any farther.

Yusuf still has my pack. He holds it out for me to take and I point to the tent, a silent plea for one last helpful gesture. He smiles and sets the pack next to the door.

"Thank you." My voice is meager and hoarse.

I slump to my knees and crawl the rest of the way to the tent. I fumble with the zipper then crawl some more, dragging the pack behind me. Sue has been waiting. I suddenly feel awkward about reaching the summit without her. I don't know what to say so I don't say anything as I collapse onto my sleeping bag.

"So." I can't read Sue's tone. "How was it?"

Chapter 30

I lack the mental energy to filter my end of the conversation. "I made it to the top. Now I can't move."

Sue shifts to the bottom of my sleeping bag. "Let me take off your boots."

I manage a smile and close my eyes, behind them a montage of moments—sharing latkes and donuts, cancer stories, a church pew, countless trails—that brought us to this spot at the top of a mountain halfway around the world.

Sue takes off my gaiters. She unties one boot, then gently slips it off.

I'm asleep before she gets to the other one.

After our post-summit nap, which felt more to me like a prolonged blink, the Lemosho clan devours Raziki's chicken and plantain stew before descending all the way back down to 10,039 feet.

We're now at Mweka Camp on the edge of the rainforest. I still haven't had a chance to talk at length with Sue about the summit, and that's bothering me. She wasn't in our tent when I woke up from my nap, and for some reason I didn't wind up next to her at lunch or on the trail.

And she isn't around now.

The good news is that Todd, who was waiting for us here, was able to recover and looks healthy.

Chapter 31

Today is the final day on the mountain.
I wake at Mweka Camp as the sun rises. Ice covers the tent and ravens call to each other in throaty croaks overhead.

I climbed Kilimanjaro yesterday.

"Climbed" is such a beautiful past-tense word.

Most of us made it to Uhuru Peak. Everyone but Todd and Sue made it to Stella Point.

I still haven't talked with Sue. She had to pack up her sleeping bag last night to be with someone at the Machame camp who was sick enough to require medical attention. We weren't given details. I'm playing the odds game and setting aside worries that it was Jim. I know Sue is needed elsewhere, but I'm anxious to clear the air. She may be nothing but happy for me. I just need to know there are no hard feelings between us.

I swap yesterday's hiking clothes with this morning's hiking clothes and set my packed bag outside the tent for the porters one last time. The days of hearing *pole, pole* are over. We've been cruising down the mountain, although my knees might benefit from slowing down. Only four hours at the most until we're off the trail for good—a little more than 4,600 feet. I tell myself it will be like a piece of chocolate cake.

We are still above the clouds, with a spectacular view of the snow-covered summit against blue skies. I overhear Alison say she needed to trade her hiking boots for regular trail sneakers because her big toes have turned a medium shade of blue. Paul is narrating one of his last videos on the trail. "We get to clean up soon and have a beer," he says. A beer sounds downright celestial right about now. Yusuf waves to the camera. "This is my favorite day of the trip," he says, "because I get paid." He laughs but by the sound of his voice, I can tell he's only half-joking.

Sue rushes back in the nick of time to pack up her things. Not wanting to hold her up, I fight back the urge to run into our tent to talk and instead stand around with the others—more than ready for our final descent. I scan faces, trying to remember the first time most of us met. It seems so long ago now that I was a nervous, grieving widow sitting down to a dinner that would change my life. I wonder whether the American Cancer Society or I wound up the worthier cause.

Then, for the last time, we hear our rallying cry. "Mohammed is ready!"

Mohammed is wearing a light blue shirt that says "Freezeroo" across the chest—the name of the annual Greater Rochester Track Club's winter road race series. I guess even lead guides need donations.

My knees carry me forward with an ardent ache into the drizzling rainforest. It has been strange, since the summit, navigating five climate zones in reverse—from the arctic to the alpine desert to the moorlands to the heather, and now back to the rainforest with its moss-covered trees, hibiscus, and log-lined trail. Soon we will be on a bus, returning to cultivated farmlands and fruit plantations, heading toward the colorful sights and commercial sounds of Moshi. It feels as if we haven't been there in weeks.

"On the right!"

I move to the left. Two porters pass carefully, carrying someone from another hiking group on a stretcher. I purposely avoid looking at the person's face. If I were in that situation, ending my journey like that, I would want to be invisible. I have every intention of ending my own journey with a hot shower.

Up ahead I see Jim on the side of the trail. We haven't had a chance to talk much one-on-one either since the summit, though last night we sat together at dinner while the entire group celebrated what we'd just accomplished. Paul had said, "Now I know why Kilimanjaro starts with 'kill-a-man'!"

I wave to Jim. "Hey there."

"Howdy. I've been waiting for you."

Jim slips into line behind me.

"All the months of preparation and now it's almost over," I say.

"Except it won't be over," he says. "This experience will always be with us."

Always with us. I like the sound of that.

We walk for a while then slow our pace to watch lead guide Mohammed pose for a picture. He crosses his arms as usual, his bald head glinting in the sun, but this time I swear I see the slightest crease of a smile on his lips.

Then, "Hey, you."

The voice is unmistakably Sue's.

I turn around and throw an arm around her. "Hey, you. Thanks again for taking off my boots."

"Well, that's what a Jewish mother does."

"I'm going to excuse myself and walk up ahead," Jim says.

I give him a grateful smile.

Sue tells me Elizabeth had been the sick one. She was disoriented and vomited seven times, and Sue had to check on her breathing throughout the night.

"She caught a cold on the plane ride over and almost stopped eating entirely by day three or four," Sue says. "She read the warning at the gate that said not to climb if you're sick, but thought, 'I didn't travel more than 7,000 miles just to turn around.'"

"I can understand that," I say.

"Rick's keeping an eye on her now."

We wind up talking more than we have on any other day on the mountain, not even pausing to put on our raincoats when it starts to sprinkle. We talk about our training, about the friendships we've made, and about perseverance, until the hours—six of them, not four—funnel themselves into our last moments on the mountain.

The end of the trail comes into view. Linda Number One is standing there, waiting for us. She starts back up the trail.

"I couldn't walk out without you two," she says.

It sounds corny but I feel like I'm on the border between now and all that is possible. I want to cry but there are too many competing emotions for the tears to spill.

The three of us link arms. We are giddy.

"We did it!" Linda Number One shouts into the calm.

"And we did it together!" I shout back.

Arm in arm, nearly skipping, we leave the mountain—and more than a year of questioning—behind us.

Chapter 32

May 2008

The canyon is arid and still, its riverbanks covered with cottonwoods, pinyon pines, and junipers. I try to spot black-chinned hummingbirds, white-throated swifts, and other desert birds known to seek shelter in crevices overhead, where a few obstinate trees cling to the sun-soaked Zion National Park bluffs.

"*Pole, pole,*" Jim says.

We are in southwest Utah on our way to Angels Landing, a steep outcropping said to be one of the National Park Service's most famous and thrilling hikes. After coming here last year, shortly after learning that my maiden name is Angel, Jim had tucked away the idea that he'd return with me someday.

My steps are slow and gentle, like careful stitching, and I remember the sense I had three months ago on Kilimanjaro—that I was being woven into a vast geological canvas.

After a pit toilet break—I'm a champ at that now—I emerge to an impressive view of Angels Landing, jutting into the middle of the canyon like a fin. Jim is talking with a middle-aged man and woman resting on a rock.

"This is the end of the trail for us," the man is saying. He points to the woman. "She's afraid of heights. She'd never do Kilimanjaro."

Jim must've mentioned our climb. I smile at the woman and take a swig from my water bottle as Jim suggests they check out the JOI website anyway.

"We should get going," Jim says. "Nice talking with you."

We wave and start walking, but Jim turns around after a few steps.

"By the way," he adds, "Kilimanjaro is way easier than the next half mile here. You won't run into anything like this over there."

I shoot Jim a nasty look. Seriously? That specific detail hadn't surfaced in any of our conversations about Angels Landing. The reading I'd done on the history of the park had been fascinating, not fear-inducing. To construct the path up to Angels Landing, horses and mules hauled equipment to workers who dangled precariously from fragile cliffs while jackhammering sandstone. Sure, Angels Landing got its name after a Methodist minister concluded that only angels could reach the top, but we'd already climbed Kilimanjaro—a place where God supposedly lives—so I hadn't foreseen any problems.

Kilimanjaro is way easier?

I take a deep breath to keep from bickering, followed by another. I love this man but how could he have kept this to himself until just now? He's a stickler for detail so it had to have been a conscious decision, which only makes me more infuriated.

After Uhuru Peak, I'm no quitter. All I can do is follow Jim, who, smart as usual, has continued walking without saying a thing. He leads the way to a thick set of chains embedded in the rock.

The metal post that anchors the chains has been knocked over.

Jim touches it with his boot. "That gives you confidence, doesn't it?"

I tighten my lips so that I can't answer. I don't have anything nice to say.

We scrabble along the sheer cliff, our fingers searching for cavities to grip. The trail is narrow and bordered by knife-edged ridges. My heart beats in my throat.

When we finally reach a flat, open area, I feel a flicker of hope. "Are we there?"

Jim chuckles and my knees buckle.

"Oh no," he says. "We have quite a ways to go yet."

I push on to another narrow sandstone ridge, this one nothing but an eight-foot spine only three feet wide in parts. More chains, these anchored more securely. The view down is harrowing—a nearly 1,200-foot drop on one side, an 800-plus-foot drop on the other. The mouth of the canyon looks hungry. I take a few steps, then a few more, holding onto the chain links for dear life. Again, I could use my triumph at Uhuru Peak to give me strength, but what do I actually need to prove? Maybe "stopping" is different than "quitting."

Without much real estate to stand on, Jim and I are shoulder to shoulder. I want to scream, or cry, or instantaneously know how to teleport. Barranco Wall was nothing compared to this. I have never been more petrified.

"We'll do whatever you want," Jim says. "I'll go in either direction with you."

I sigh, partly because I believe him, partly because I want to strangle him.

At this moment, like it or not, I do have climbing to the top of Kilimanjaro as a frame of reference. Much like with cancer, there had been a degree of surrender to the fears I'd faced in Africa. I had been scared at times for my safety—and had worried whether I would make it—but moment after moment had pushed on. The last day on the mountain I accepted an official certificate of achievement to prove it.

Jim stands still on the slim ridge. He keeps his voice steady and calm. "I know this is really hard for you. Whatever you want to do is fine with me. Really."

"OK, give me a minute."

I try not to think about the dizzying drop-offs or the fact that the park advertises its trail system as part of a "highly erosive environment." Or about having to get back down. Without a word I inch forward.

Eventually we clear the ridge and I feel that particular sense of satisfaction that comes from putting fear in its place. But there's more to go. It takes another drawn-out half hour on the rugged trail to reach the very top of Angel's Landing. Joining a sparse crowd, we relax on a flat rock and gorge on granola bars, crackers, and cheese. From our lofty perch, the views are breathtaking in every direction. There's the Great White Throne, Red Arch Mountain, Cathedral Mountain, Observation Point, Cable Mountain, Big Bend, and the Organ, a rock formation that horseshoes around the shimmering, snaking Virgin River below.

Jim stands up and slaps crumbs off his hands. "Follow me."

We walk toward a small ledge atop the towering monolith. I stop when close enough to the lip, but Jim walks ahead. Concentrating on the back of his shirt, I push away hostile thoughts about accidents. He doesn't stand at the ledge long and offers his hand when he's back at my side.

"Ready?"

I start to nod, then realize we've been at the top long enough for me to forget about what is bound to be a spine-chilling descent.

"We'll see," I answer.

I let Jim lead again, though he stops after less than a minute.

"Why don't you sit down so I can take your picture?" He points toward an area dotted with pinyon trees. "Sit next to that one with the crooked trunk."

I don't say what I'm thinking—that we just got off our rumps and I need to build momentum. Did he forget what's ahead?

Instead I sit next to the trunk, cross my ankles, and grasp my shin.

"Nice."

Click.

I bend forward to stand up. By the time I'm fully upright, Jim is in front of me with tears in his eyes, his lips pressed together. He takes my hands. My stomach sinks. I wonder what's wrong but stay quiet so I can listen to what he has to say.

He just stands there, looking at me.

I squeeze his hands.

He opens his mouth. "I love you very much."

I'm confused. "I love you too."

"I want to spend the rest of my life with you. Will you marry me?"

I start to cry.

My voice quivers when I answer. "Yes. I would be honored to marry you."

We hug for a long time.

I look at the sky over Jim's shoulder. *Bill, I'm so incredibly grateful to you for bringing Jim into my life.*

For a split second I think of Sister Dorothy, about an exchange we once had before she left for vacation. Jim and I had only been on a few dates. "Don't get married while I'm in Ireland," she said. "We're just dating," I shot back. It had been a big step for me to add a picture of Jim and myself—together—to the montage on my refrigerator and Sister Dorothy had noticed. But the idea of becoming someone else's bride, ever, was ludicrous. I didn't think anyone could ever care about me as deeply as Bill had.

"Oh my God!" Now I'm shrieking. "I mean...oh my God!"

Jim laughs. "I know we're both really excited, but we still have to get down. We need to concentrate."

He doesn't need to worry about me. I have no qualms about the descent anymore, though I wind up holding onto the chains even tighter than on the way up—not out of fear so much as a feeling I might float away.

Chapter 33

Two months after our engagement, Jim decides to sell his house. He figures if he puts it on the market in July, fingers crossed, it will sell by the wedding in November. But the house has been on the market only 45 minutes when the real estate agent shows up with a middle-aged woman and her mother, who take a tour and give him an offer a few minutes after they leave.

Days later, at my house, Jim asks, "Would you like me to get an apartment until we're married? Maybe I could find something right around here."

It is so thoughtful, so old-fashioned and polite, so completely unnecessary.

"I'm comfortable with you moving in," I say.

I mean it but can't help thinking about Bill's side of the bedroom closet. Empty the last three years.

With Jim moving in, I put a little extra elbow grease into my next cleaning—polishing the wood furniture with lemon oil and making sure pictures of both families are spread around the house. I move from room to room at a good clip until I get to my bedroom. Soon to be our bedroom.

Sitting on the edge of the bed I stare at the smudges on the mirror and fidget with a wet paper towel. Just because you wipe something away doesn't mean you erase it, I say to myself over and over, waiting for the repetition to turn into permission to do what I need to do.

I've gotten used to the differences between Jim and Bill, such as how Jim lounges around the house in T-shirts with armpit holes, something Bill wouldn't have tolerated. And I appreciate how Jim has shown he can consider another man's home his own. He knows I'm not forgetting Bill—he even cleared an area near the driveway, between a handful of mature beech trees, for the hammock Bill had gotten as a gift but never hung. He has been exceptionally supportive since he leaned forward for our first sustained kiss, soft and slow. That night, at dinner overlooking Seneca Lake, Jim talked about his divorce and two grown kids. I talked mostly about Michelle. When he sensed me hesitating after starting a story that involved Bill, he encouraged me to continue, prodding me with questions until I finished.

I walk to the mirror and move the paper towel slowly, painstakingly, over the glass—rocking my body with every stroke, rubbing the smudges until the only thing left is my unblemished reflection.

Chapter 34

Katie and I stand at the back of the church. Clutching a bouquet of muted fall flowers, I rest my free hand on her shoulder as I move my gaze from one pew to the next, to rows of beaming faces that have seen me through calamity and convalescence.

Almost four years after Bill's death and six months from the day Jim proposed, it's time to walk down the aisle. My mouth is dry. I haven't allowed myself anything to drink since leaving the house hours ago, afraid of fighting a needy bladder in the middle of my vows. I suck the moisture from my tongue.

The overcast morning already is a blur. I'd had my makeup done at the hairdresser's to save time, including a touch-up job to cover the permanent black dots on my chest, the pinpoint tattoos once used for radiation treatments. Afterward, in my bedroom, Michelle helped me into my wedding dress—an ivory, sleeveless V-neck with alternating layers of satin and chiffon. I put on the Connemara marble necklace and matching earrings Jim gave me for Christmas, then a small, understated crown and gold shoes. I held Michelle's hands. "We've been through a lot, and I'm really happy we can share this day," I'd said. "Thanks for being here."

There wasn't time to hang onto the words. Katie, running into the room in her chocolate-brown velvet dress and matching jacket, was shouting, "The photographer's here!"

In the closest row I catch sight of the Bible verse I chose for the program's back cover:

> *Love*
> *Bears all things*
> *Believes all things*
> *Hopes all things*
> *Endures all things*

Jim smiles at me from the end of an aisle so short, I had asked the organist to play Pachelbel's "Canon in D" more slowly than usual for my walk to the front of the church. I'm curious how my soon-to-be husband is doing. The poor guy. He was so teary during the rehearsal, the pastor put an arm around me and wondered aloud, "How is the groom going to make it through the ceremony?"

I look at my engagement ring. Jim hadn't given me one when he proposed, assuming I'd want to have a say in what it looked like. He was right. Instead of shopping around, I asked for his blessing to keep the setting from my twentieth wedding anniversary band and substitute the diamonds on each side for tanzanite, the deep-blue gemstones from East Africa. It was a way for me to honor a past I don't need to cling to or forget about, a past that makes me who I am—and that ultimately led me to Jim. "Of course," he'd said.

When we exchange vows I will say, "We have many times spoken of another who has given me to you. We will accept this and trust that he and our Lord have placed us in their tender hands and graced us with infinite love."

Sister Dorothy gets my attention with a small wave and gives me a knowing glance. She'd written Jim and me a wedding prayer:

Chapter 34

Ever loving God, our hearts are filled with gratitude, love, and friendship.
As these two lives merge into one path, we ask you to take Bonnie and Jim into your loving arms.
Care for them as they have cared and shared with each of us.
Keep a loving eye on them.
Grant them joyful hours, days, and years.
May the mountains they encounter be small.
May their joys and love reach beyond the heights of Mt. Kilimanjaro.
Bless us all as we celebrate with them today.
Amen.

We liked the prayer so much, we had it printed on cream cardstock to include with each place setting at the reception.

Piano music starts and a deep voice fills the church. "Drink to me only with thine eyes…And I will pledge with mine…"

Michelle, along with Jim's two children, light memorial candles. Michelle is wearing one of the necklaces I gave her and Beth two days ago—pendants made with the diamonds from my anniversary band.

With the candles lit, "Canon in D" brings everyone to their feet.

All eyes are on me.

I lock mine with Jim's.

Standing here in a wedding dress instead of hiking pants, I could say the same words I offered when Paul videotaped me on that second day on the mountain.

"I'm not sure what I hoped for, but it's definitely more than I ever imagined."

Epilogue

For 16 days we've fought the bleary-eyed fatigue that is customary on trips with Rick, passing through villages and walking on trails used daily by the people, cows, and horses of Nepal. Only one day to go before we are on a jetliner back to New York, watching in-flight movies and having convenient access to a bathroom, the sound of yak bells to be heard only in our dreams.

Ten of the 12 of us here climbed Mount Kilimanjaro together. On our second day I caught my first glimpse of Mount Everest, framed between leafy trees. The sun was lustrous on the snowy peaks. The mountain stayed in sight for the most part as we moved higher into the Himalayas, past ancient lake beds and up steep switchbacks to Kala Patthar, at an elevation of around 18,500 feet.

Two years ago we had stood on the "Roof of Africa." Kala Patthar is known as the "Roof of the World."

This trip has turned out to be much harder physically than Kilimanjaro had been—with substantially more high-altitude hiking days. We have walked between six and 12 miles each day. I've lagged toward the end of the line, and Jim has moved between the front and back, as usual.

This afternoon, under brilliant blue skies and about six hours into the day's trek, we're navigating a steep part of a trail between Khumjung and Monjo. The scree makes every step arduous. My body wants to retaliate, the weariness feeling like a grudge I can't shake. Like on Kilimanjaro, it's about focusing on one step at a time.

Left foot, right foot, on and on, until I slip on a mix of loose stones and dirt. I land solidly on the ground like a cheerleader—left leg forward, right leg bent backward at the knee. The swelling around my right knee starts immediately, as do the tears.

Catching my breath, I double over and grip my kneecap.

Kami, the Sherpa guiding the group, appears within seconds. In one fluid motion he repositions my bent leg and massages my knee, the swollen shape like a head of cauliflower. Kami's touch is delicate. I don't want to watch the swelling so I stare at Kami's veiny hands, then at the broken veins around his slight cheekbones under a soft, sparse beard. His peach button-down shirt is tucked carelessly into his pants. Kami comes from a prominent family in Khumjung, one of the area's more prosperous towns. We stayed in Khumjung last night, and came away so impressed by the green tin roofs and electric street lights that we dubbed it the Aspen, Colorado of the Himalayas. We slept in tents in a fog-laden potato field outside the house that has been in his family for generations. Even with his affluence, Kami wears the same pants and baseball cap every day. I try to let that paradox distract me as he puts a little more weight behind his strokes.

These stupid knees. I've had meniscus surgery on each one over the last year. Before leaving for Mount Everest I was interrogated by my physical therapist, starting with, "What the hell are you thinking?"

Now, seemingly stranded on the highest mountain on earth, I have a question of my own. Am I going to have to be evacuated?

Then, at last, Jim is here.

"Hey." He rubs my shoulder. "What happened?"

I close my eyes and shake my head, too frustrated to explain.

This adventure had been my idea. After Kilimanjaro and Zion National Park, at the annual reunion party for Pack, Paddle, Ski clients, Rick stood on a table to announce he'd started planning another one of his Everest trips. I whipped my head around at Jim, my brows lifted with hope. "Wanna do this? We can do this, right?" I pleaded. Not as spontaneous as I am, Jim hesitated, his analytical mind first needing to map out finances before making a commitment. But he came around quickly. We celebrated our second wedding anniversary with the other hikers the day we landed in Kathmandu.

Kami stops the rubbing. He looks at me, not saying anything, waiting for me to assess where I stand—and if I can stand—with my bloated knee. A group of boys in red sweaters and dark pants, carrying backpacks, pass by on their way home from school. A group of girls in red sweaters and dark skirts follows. I watch their legs scissor in the sunlight, casting stark shadows onto the dirt.

Turning onto my palms and knees, I wince as I push myself up, careful not to put too much weight on my right leg. Jim dusts off my pants.

I pull from my past.

I can do this.

I take in the thorny trail ahead—the rocks that poke through the soil, the sticks that cluster around tattered tree roots.

"You ready?" Jim asks.

I nod, feeling tenacious as the terrain.

A note from Robin L. Flanigan

I looked like a walking question mark, slogging up Mount Kilimanjaro after five days on the trail. I hadn't slept a wink the past two nights and hadn't been able to eat more than a few bites of bread in three days. After collapsing onto a rock, I implored a guide to sing to me. I needed my attention on something other than my pain—something sentimental and comforting. Back on my feet, in the dark, it was easy to let the sound of his voice become the center of attention. I focused on the row of reflective strips along the hem of his pants, gleaming from my headlamp.

Bonnie, a two-time cancer survivor, walked ahead of me. Nearly 40 of us were on this mountain to celebrate life after treatment—ours or someone else's—while raising money and awareness for cancer research.

Everyone on our trek up Kilimanjaro, like most anyone who has been through cancer, had a similar tale of shock and resolve. I had heard little about Bonnie's background but enough to know she had a heavier load to carry than many of us. After becoming a sudden widow three years earlier, she had signed up for the climb to help push past her grief and return to the adventurous life she once shared with her husband. It was the kind of inspiring story that appealed to a journalist like me. Over the course of my career I have found myself drawn to stories involving tragic circumstances, intrigued by all the ways people work through their pain. I have spent months with some of them, chronicling their grief and recovery for publication, wondering years later whether my interest helped or harmed them in the end. But not once over our year of training for Kilimanjaro, or during our time in Tanzania, did I think about asking Bonnie to let me interview her.

Seven months after returning from Africa—nudged, over a

Saturday morning breakfast, by someone who knows me well—I decided to abandon an in-progress memoir about five years of infertility tests, treatments, and failed pregnancies. Writing about those experiences was keeping my anguish alive instead of providing closure. What if I wrote about what Bonnie had been through instead? An interesting thought, but I felt uneasy about asking her to relive the bitter minutiae of her experience. For an audience, no less. Wasn't that exactly what I was trying to escape by wanting to ditch my memoir?

I called her anyway, two days later, just before leaving for work. After some nervous rambling—I would've sounded more awkward with a prepared script—there was silence. When Bonnie finally spoke, she said, "On Saturday morning, probably around the time you were having breakfast, I was praying aloud. I said, 'I don't know how, but it's time to tell my story.' You just opened my heart. God has brought you to me."

Somehow my act of feared selfishness had been transformed into divine intervention. I cried. I was more relieved than surprised by her answer. The truth is, in my experience, relationships seem to form when they're needed—and it turned out we needed each other.

In the journal Bonnie kept on Kilimanjaro, she wrote that her changes could lead others to their own changes: "What a wonderful thing to recognize…What a gift!…A responsibility to hold close to my heart, to protect and take very seriously." She may not have envisioned a book when she wrote those words, but she felt compelled to share her story in some way—and I relate to that. I have written essays and given interviews about my experiences with infertility for the same reason, to connect with people who might draw strength from the ways I have found purpose out of the seemingly pointless.

Bonnie is the strongest woman I have ever met and one of my greatest teachers. She has made it safe for me to question the exquisite complications of life, even in the midst of celebrating

Afterword

them. I look at her and see irrefutable proof that hope and healing are intertwined and can lead to extraordinary things.

The two of us struggled together on the mountain, though I purposely left myself out of this story because I wanted it to be hers alone. And we struggled together on another journey—this book—with me pushing for haunting details and with her needing periods of long, painful reflection. Both journeys have been deep and abiding and have linked us as women convinced that one person's vulnerability is another person's strength.

We hope that strength finds those who need it.

On to the next adventure.

Kwa moyo wote
(with my whole heart),
Robin L. Flanigan

Giving Back

Journeys of Solutions, Inc. formed out of Journeys of Inspiration in the spring of 2008.

Because travelers often return home from a developing country with a desire to help the people and communities they've encountered, the nonprofit organization provides assistance with launching grassroots projects, fundraising, and the logistics of working internationally. Projects often involve infrastructure improvements, education, and health care.

To find out more, or to make a donation, please visit www.journeysofsolutions.org

Acknowledgments

To my climber companions,
    I am humbled by, and filled with gratitude for, the continued support and love you each show to me and to one another.

With abundant love,
Bonnie

Made in the USA
Middletown, DE
07 June 2024